Graham MacGregor, MD, is Senior Lecturer and Honorary Consultant Physician in the Department of Medicine of Charing Cross Hospital Medical School in London. He is Director of the Blood Pressure Unit at Charing Cross Hospital and has many years' experience of treating patients with high blood pressure. His major research interest has been into the mechanisms involved in the development of high blood pressure and, in particular, the role of salt. The Blood Pressure Unit was the first to demonstrate unequivocally that moderate reduction of salt intake does lower blood pressure in many patients with high blood pressure.

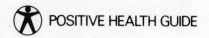
POSITIVE HEALTH GUIDE

THE SALT-FREE DIET BOOK

*An appetizing way to help reduce
high blood pressure*

Graham MacGregor, MD

Foreword by Norman M Kaplan, MD
Professor of Internal Medicine, University of Texas

Arco Publishing, Inc.
New York

To my wife Christiane, whose invaluable help made this book
possible

Published 1985 by Arco Publishing, Inc.
215 Park Avenue South, New York, N.Y. 10003

First published in the United Kingdom in 1984
by Martin Dunitz Ltd, London

Library of Congress Cataloging in Publication Data
MacGregor,Graham.
  The salt-free diet book
  (Positive health guide)
  Includes index.
  1. Hypertension—Prevention.   2. Hypertension—Diet therapy.   3. Salt-free
diet—Recipes.
I. Title.   II. Series.
RC685.H8M23   1985   613.2′8   84-2813
ISBN 0-668-05972-9 (softcover)

North American dietetic consultant: Karen Gunner BSc MSc, PDt
North American editorial consultant: Lee Faber

Phototypeset in Garamond by Book Ens, Saffron Walden, England

Printed by Toppan Printing Company (S) Pte Ltd, Singapore

Front cover photograph shows: Leeks vinaigrette (top, see page 50), Chili con
carne (center right, see page 74), Spaghetti with pesto sauce (bottom, see page
51).
Back cover photograph shows: Orange chocolate cake (top, see page 84),
Orange and date fruit salad (center and bottom, see page 84).

CONTENTS

FOREWORD

Norman M. Kaplan, Professor of Internal Medicine, Hypertension Section,
University of Texas Health Science Center/Southwestern Medical School, Dallas, Texas

We are, all of us, eating too much sodium, far beyond what nature intended for us. As Dr MacGregor clearly documents in this book, this excessive amount of sodium is likely involved in causing hypertension, the most common and serious risk for heart attacks and strokes. If that were not enough, other common problems, from premenstrual tension to heart failure, are also shown to be aggravated by the taste for sodium that we acquire early in life.

In the last few years, medical science and public pressure have combined to increase awareness of the problem of excess sodium. As a result, governmental regulations are being formulated to require the labelling of the sodium content of processed foods, more and more food processors are making lower sodium foods available, and more and more of us are cutting down on our sodium intake.

But the battle has only been joined. A great deal more needs to be done, from cutting down the sodium content of babies' diets, to preparing tasty alternatives to high-sodium foods, and providing lower-sodium snacks and fast foods.

Dr Graham MacGregor has written this short book to provide needed ammunition in the broadening attempts by all of us – health profession and general public – to remove the burden of heavy sodium intake. As a leading investigator of both basic and applied aspects of the sodium relationship to hypertension, he is uniquely equipped to expose the problems. As a gifted user of language, he has done an excellent job of making things simple – but not superficial.

To read and assimilate the background of the sodium issue as presented in the earlier sections of this book will take some time and effort. But it explains the concerns that more and more of us have about excess sodium and justifies the preparation and use of a lower sodium–higher potassium diet. The latter part of the book provides general and specific information on preparing tasty and attractive lower-sodium foods and drinks. The information is explicit and the recipes and menus look inviting. All in all, this will be a useful guide-book in the growing effort to overcome an important problem in the public's health. I welcome Dr MacGregor's contribution and hope that all of us will heed his good advice.

INTRODUCTION:
Who needs a
salt-free diet?

Nutritional experts throughout the world are now recommending a reduction in salt intake for the whole population and particularly for those people who have high blood pressure. High blood pressure leads to strokes and heart attacks and is probably one of the most preventable causes of death in the Western world.

This book explains how salt in small amounts is necessary in our bodies and how too much can be harmful for those who already have high blood pressure or heart problems and perhaps for healthy people too. There are many ways of cutting down your salt intake but it is really easy when you know where the salt is in the food you eat.

The first part of the book shows what quantities you should be aiming for and how it can be done. You will soon learn to enjoy the taste of less salty, but attractively flavored foods. The recipes were developed on this basis and as you try them out, I am sure you will agree that the real reason to reduce your salt intake is that natural good food tastes better without it.

Salt – what is it?

Although salt is the chemical name for many substances made up of crystals, when the word salt is mentioned we all think of table salt or the salt that is put on the roads, and that is of course the type we are describing in the book. Known as sodium chloride, it is made up of approximately 40 per cent sodium and 60 per cent chloride. Salt is the main source of sodium in the Western diet, but some other foods contain it in other forms, for example, the sodium bicarbonate in baking powder, which is used in baking cookies and cakes. But for simplicity many people refer to salt when in fact they mean sodium, and vice versa.

Sodium's vital role in the body
All the cells that make up our body are bathed in a fluid which contains sodium and chloride in solution, that is, a salt solution. The concentration of sodium in this fluid is very carefully regulated by

the body and is approximately the same as the sodium that was in the sea when life emerged onto land many millions of years ago. The sea now contains more sodium because of erosion of the land by rain over the last few million years, which has washed sodium down into the sea. Sodium and chloride are vital for both the working of the body cells and in regulating the volume of blood and fluid around them.

The body is made up of millions of little cells surrounded by fluid containing sodium. Inside these cells there is very little sodium whereas there is a large amount of another mineral, potassium. The outer covering or membrane of the cell allows both potassium and sodium to pass through it. As sodium is in much greater concentration outside the cell, there is a continuous tendency for it to move in and, as potassium is in a greater concentration inside the cell, there is a tendency for it to come out. To maintain the balance between sodium outside the cell and potassium inside, there is a sodium-potassium pump on the membrane which is continuously pumping sodium out as potassium is pumped into the cell. This sodium-potassium pump is vital to the proper functioning of body cells. It is now thought that this sodium pump could play an important role in regulating blood pressure (see below).

Fluid retention
The amount of sodium in your body affects the volume of fluid bathing the tissues. If a large amount of sodium is eaten, the body retains some of it and water stays with it, so that the volume of fluid in the body increases. This can be clearly seen if you increase sodium intake from a very low amount, say 10 mmol (0.25 g) per day, to a high amount of about 250 mmol (6 g) per day (see page 22 for an explanation of measurements). The increase in sodium intake causes fluid retention, making a weight gain of around 1½ kg (3 lb). A reduction of sodium intake from a very high level to a low level will cause a loss of sodium and therefore of water. With this fluid loss there will be a loss of weight. Many crash diets use this principle. For instance, if you do not eat for a few days, you will consume no sodium and there will be an initial loss of weight. However, this is not due to loss of fat but only of body fluid, which is immediately regained if more sodium is eaten.

How do we regulate the sodium content of the body?
The amount of sodium in the body is a balance between the amount eaten, nearly all of which is absorbed into the body, and the amount removed by the kidneys into the urine. The way the kidney acts in getting rid of sodium and maintaining the balance is very complex. When we eat more sodium, there is an increase both in the sodium and the fluid inside the body until the body's mechanisms, mainly regulated by hormones (messengers in the blood), come in. They cause loss of more sodium in the urine and a

new balance is obtained at a slightly higher fluid level in the whole body.

How much sodium or salt do we actually need?

During evolution and even in some societies today, humans were dependent for sodium on fruits and vegetables and the occasional meal of meat or fish, which had a slightly higher sodium content. Clearly, humans were able to survive on this very low sodium diet partly because of the kidney's incredible ability to hold on to sodium when it is in short supply in the diet. Studies on Indian tribes in the Venezuelan jungle have shown how well we are adapted to a very low sodium diet. Measurement of these tribes and estimates of our ancestors over the last million years indicate that natural sodium intake is approximately between 0.5 and 10 mmol per day (10 to 250 mg per day).

With increasing civilization, salt could be obtained either by evaporating sea water or by mining it. It was found that it had the almost magical property of preserving food. This was particularly important in the winter and, not surprisingly, salt which had nearly always been in short supply, became highly valued. Indeed, Roman soldiers were partly paid in salt, hence the word 'salary'. At the same time as preserving food, salt was thought to purify it, and for this reason it took on religious as well as economic importance.

With our recent ability to produce salt very cheaply, and since we've found other ways of preserving food, its value has lessened considerably, although as a chemical, salt is still very important.

Sodium is often in short supply in animals and more primitive human communities, and they have a strong salt appetite seen, for example, in deer or cattle going to salt licks. In the West our sodium intake is so high that we have no such craving for salt. But as a result of habit over the last two or three hundred years, we have become used to eating a very large amount. The average consumption of sodium in the West is around 120 to 250 mmol of sodium per day, or 8 to 14 g of sodium chloride per day (for a fuller explanation of how sodium is measured see page 22). There is now general agreement that this is far too much but little on how much we should be eating.

The very low amounts of sodium eaten by primitive man are not, at the present time, practical in the West unless tremendous care is taken with the diet. Even if they were, an intake of around 1 mmol per day could be dangerous if there was a big loss of body fluids due to diarrhea or severe vomiting. However, most experts would agree that cutting the amount by about half to around 60 to 80 mmol of sodium per day would be a sensible compromise for the present. Remember that this is still five to ten times more than was eaten during the last million years of our evolution. It is easy to reduce sodium intake to this amount and, in our experience, most people taking the diet up have found it a lot more enjoyable than their previous high-salt diet.

Why is too much salt harmful?

A high-salt consumption can be harmful in several conditions, but by far the most important effect is on blood pressure, and this may lead to serious disease.

High blood pressure

Six out of ten of us will die from some disorder of the small blood vessels that supply oxygen and essential nutrients to the tissues. These small blood vessels called arteries, and the even smaller ones, which are called arterioles, become narrowed and scarred with fatty deposits as we grow older. This is known as atheroma or arteriosclerosis. The scarring and narrowing of the arteries is directly responsible for strokes or cerebrovascular accidents, heart attacks and some forms of kidney disease. Arterial disease may also affect arteries in the limbs and in particular the blood supply to the legs.

Clearly, an understanding of the cause of this arterial disease would result in a major improvement in health and an increase in life expectancy. Studies from all over the world looking at different communities have shown that there are three important factors that make it much more likely for someone to develop arterial disease and therefore to die of a stroke or heart attack. These are:

1. High blood pressure
2. High saturated fat intake
3. Smoking.

While the increased danger of developing arterial disease with any of these conditions has been proved, and of course the risks are greater when two or all three factors are involved, we still need more direct evidence that reducing the risks will reduce the number of strokes and heart attacks. It is now known that lowering blood pressure and cutting out smoking improve people's chances, but we are less certain about the effect of lowering saturated fat intake – although there is some evidence that lowering it reduces the risks of getting a heart attack.

Many people find giving up cigarette smoking extremely difficult, however important it is for their health. Lowering blood pressure either with pills or by other means is much easier, so at present, high blood pressure is probably the most preventable cause of death in the Western world.

What is blood pressure?

This is the pressure of the blood in the arteries. Blood is pumped through the arteries, capillaries and veins by the heart contracting. When the heart contracts, the pressure of the blood in the arteries rises to a peak, called the systolic pressure, and when the heart relaxes, the pressure in the arteries falls but not down to zero because the arteries are elastic and have some recoil. This lower pressure when the heart is relaxed is known as diastolic pressure.

How is it measured?
Blood pressure can be measured in any artery in the body but the easiest way is with a cuff that can be inflated around the arm. The cuff is filled with air to a pressure above the pressure of blood in the artery so that no blood goes into the lower arm. Then the cuff is slowly deflated and blood flows back into the arm. Measurement is by a column of mercury expressed as the height of the column in millimetres (mmHg). We find the height at the systolic pressure by listening through a stethoscope to the flow of blood below the cuff. At the systolic pressure the flow in the artery will be disturbed by the cuff and sounds will be heard through the stethoscope.

Systolic pressure can be more easily, but less accurately, measured by feeling for the pulse beat as the cuff is deflated.

When the pressure of the cuff reaches diastolic pressure, the flow in the arteries is less disturbed and the sounds heard with the stethoscope disappear, so we are able to measure the diastolic pressure as well.

What is a normal blood pressure?
Everyone's blood pressure is variable. It is lowest during sleep, when the muscles are relaxed, and high during mental or physical activity or periods of anxiety. It even varies according to whether you're standing or sitting. However, for practical reasons doctors have arrived at blood pressure measurements that they consider normal and abnormal, depending on age and other factors. So we can get a rough idea of the state of any one person's blood pressure. In relaxed conditions, for an average person, a systolic pressure above 160 mmHg or a diastolic pressure above 90 mmHg is said to be abnormal. We write this as 160/90 mmHg. Using this measurement, around 20 per cent or one person in five of the population in the West has high blood pressure.

How do you know if you have high blood pressure?
There are no symptoms. The only way of knowing what your blood pressure is, is to have it measured. If you do not know it, why not have it done now? Knowing it is probably just as important if not a lot more so than knowing your weight. Keeping your blood pressure down will largely prevent the far too common complications of high blood pressure, particularly strokes.

How does salt raise blood pressure?
Studies in animals have shown that the higher the salt intake, the higher the blood pressure. As it is not possible to do similar experiments on humans, we have to rely on more circumstantial evidence from studying different communities. Comparing salt

intake in primitive communities, where very little sodium is eaten, with countries in the West, where much more sodium is eaten, has shown that there is a direct relationship between salt intake in a particular community and the number of people in that community with high blood pressure. The table below gives an idea of the levels in the different communities.

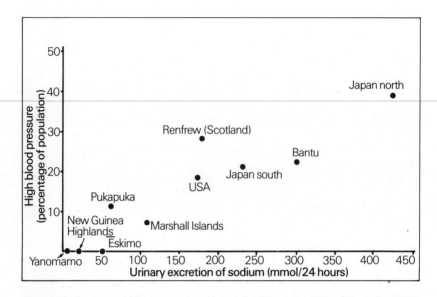

There is general agreement that in the majority of people who are going to develop or have developed high blood pressure, there is an inherited abnormality of the kidney which is responsible. But the effect of this abnormality has been a puzzle for some time. It could be that there is a difficulty in getting rid of sodium. If this were so, people with high blood pressure on a high-sodium diet would retain slightly more fluid inside the body, and some years ago this was thought by many to be a cause of high blood pressure. But as we now know, the majority of people with high blood pressure have the same amount of fluid in the blood and around their tissues as people with normal blood pressure, so an increase in fluid could not be the direct cause.

A more recent suggestion is that the defect in the kidney's ability to get rid of sodium causes an increase in a sodium excreting hormone in an attempt to overcome the abnormality. It would seem that this increased sodium excreting hormone is largely successful in getting rid of the extra sodium in the body, but as a side effect it might slow down sodium pumps, not only in the kidney, but also in the cell membranes, particularly in the little cells surrounding the arterioles, which are more contracted in people with high blood pressure. There is now some evidence to support this theory: the pumps are slower in people with high blood pressure. When the sodium pumps are slowed, the cells around the arteries contract and the arteries narrow. The result is a greater resistance to flow, and after a while there is a rise in the pressure of blood trying to move into these little arteries. High blood pressure seems therefore to be caused both by an inherited abnormality of the kidney and, more importantly as it can be changed, the amount of sodium in the diet.

Does reducing sodium intake prevent the development of high blood pressure?   Tests on animals that would normally develop high blood pressure show a reduction of sodium intake will nearly always prevent the condition. There have been no similar tests done on humans and such evidence is unlikely to be available for many years; although one study on newborn babies done in Holland in 1983 showed that a group fed on a low sodium diet for one year had lower blood pressure than a similar group fed on a normal sodium diet. Doctors now generally agree that people who have a family history of high blood pressure, strokes and heart attacks should cut back on their sodium intake as it seems that this group particularly is at risk. Whether everyone should cut down on sodium is more open to argument (see page 20).

Does reducing sodium intake lower blood pressure when it is already raised?   There is no doubt that this is so. About forty years ago, before pills were developed, high blood pressure was treated by cutting out salt almost entirely. Very low sodium diets were effective, but many people found them monotonous and difficult to stick to. Much more exciting is the recent realization that a less drastic reduction of sodium, to around half of what we now eat, does lower blood pressure to about the same extent as taking a single blood pressure lowering pill each day. Although this does not always cure blood pressure when it is already raised, it can be very helpful even for people with mildly raised blood pressure, when pills are not considered necessary.

Other studies have also shown that cutting sodium intake by half does improve the action of blood pressure lowering pills if you are already on them. The higher the blood pressure the more effective the restriction of sodium.

If you have high blood pressure and you do decide to cut back on your sodium intake, it is a good idea to discuss this with your doctor. In some people, particularly those on a very high sodium intake, it may have a marked blood pressure lowering effect and it may sometimes be possible to stop one of the pills that you are on, particularly the diuretic pills, but this should never be done without consulting your doctor.

What else can you do if you have high blood pressure?

1.   Many studies have shown that if you are overweight and you reduce your weight to normal, this will cause the blood pressure to fall.

2. If you smoke, it is extremely important to stop. This will, in itself, reduce the risk of a heart attack and to a lesser extent, the risk of a stroke, as well as reducing the danger of developing lung cancer.

3. Excessive amounts of alcohol have recently been shown to increase blood pressure very considerably, particularly the day after drinking large quantities. It is sensible therefore to not drink excessively. Intake should be restricted to an average of one to two drinks a day, that is, ¼ to ½ a liter (1 to 2 glasses) of beer, one to two glasses of wine or one to two measures of liquor.

4. *Other dietary factors: potassium*   Increasing potassium intake may lower blood pressure and as potassium is mainly present in fruit and vegetables, it is a good idea to increase consumption of these foods. Besides, eating more fruit and vegetables helps to reduce sodium intake and at the same time decreases the amount of saturated fat in the diet, as well as increasing the fiber content. (For further details on potassium, see page 28.)
    Fat   All nutritional experts recommend a reduction in total fat intake, and a switch from saturated fats (mainly but not invariably animal fat) to fats rich in polyunsaturates, eg, corn oil, sunflower oil (see page 29).
    Other minerals   There is some work suggesting that taking extra magnesium and calcium may regulate blood pressure. However, at present the evidence is too confused to allow any general recommendation to be made.

5. Regular exercise or keeping fit makes you feel better and may lower blood pressure.

6. The usual assumption is that the more relaxed you are, the lower your blood pressure will be. There is no doubt that when you are asleep your blood pressure falls (see page 13). Your muscles relax and the pressure drops. Most relaxation techniques such as biofeedback, yoga and meditation are based on this physiological reflex and may lower blood pressure during the relaxation.
    However, we are not able to say for certain that blood pressure is lower after you have finished a period of relaxation, and there is no direct evidence that a hectic, stressed lifestyle contributes to high blood pressure. But it is sensible to relax as much as possible as undue stress is no fun. Try to achieve a proper balance, though, not to be so relaxed that you get bored!

Sodium intake in other situations

While high blood pressure is the biggest danger to people eating a lot of salt, there are other reasons that make cutting down important, even in the youngest age groups.

Babies and young children

The kidneys of young babies are not able to handle the amounts of sodium that adults can. In the 1960s, milk powder for feeding babies contained too much sodium. Many were at risk from developing a high level of sodium in the fluid around their tissues. Fortunately, this was realized and the amount of sodium in milk powder was reduced, although even now, when properly made up, it still contains more sodium than human milk. At the same time as the amount of sodium in milk powder was reduced, so was the quantity in baby foods. But recent studies have shown that mothers often make the milk formula too concentrated, and in preparing other foods for babies, they tend to add salt to their own taste and end up with a diet that contains more sodium than the manufactured food. It is very important to follow the instructions exactly when making up milk formula and not to use too much. You should not add salt to food that is being prepared for babies.

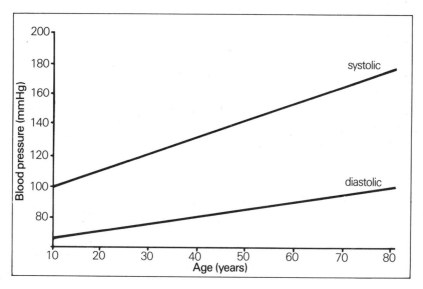

Most preschool and young schoolchildren are eating foods with a very high sodium content. Many young children exist almost entirely on processed snacks and other foods very high in sodium – and fat – for example, potato chips, cookies and hamburgers. A study from Australia showed that preschool children are eating as much sodium as adults, although their kidneys cannot cope with the same quantity.

The food that children eat largely determines the food they eat later in life. There is great concern amongst many nutritionists that the next generation, because of the much higher sodium intake that they become used to at a young age, will produce an even greater number of people with high blood pressure than in the present adult population. Certainly, it would be a good idea to guide our children to eat a more healthful diet, particularly to eat more fresh fruit and vegetables rather than the processed snacks, candies and fast foods that they eat so often now.

Sodium and premenstrual swelling

Nearly all women have experienced a gain in weight and a feeling of bloatedness before their periods. Many get these symptoms at other times. The exact cause of this retention of sodium and water is not clear, although the premenstrual swelling is likely to be due to the hormonal changes that occur during the menstrual cycle. The most common symptoms are a bloated feeling, swelling of the abdomen and sometimes swelling of the ankles and fingers, particularly noticed on the ring fingers. If these symptoms are bad, women are treated with diuretics, pills that cause the kidney to lose more sodium and water. The swelling will temporarily go down. Unfortunately, these pills have many longterm side effects and do, though rarely, cause such conditions as diabetes and gout. More importantly, they only temporarily relieve the swelling. At times they can actually increase it by making the body try to compensate so that when the diuretic is stopped, there is greater retention of sodium and water. This often leads to a vicious circle where women are advised by their doctor to stop the diuretics but find that as soon as they do, they swell up badly. This can give the mistaken idea that they really need these pills.

A more logical way of treating any swelling of this kind is to reduce the amount of salt or sodium in the diet. The less sodium you eat, the less fluid will be locked into the body. As well as cutting back on salt, another helpful move is to eat more potassium as this helps the body to get rid of sodium and so lose the extra fluid (see pages 14, 28). Our experience with women who have very bad swelling and who have been on diuretic pills for many years is that if they restrict their sodium intake, following the ways outlined in this book, and at the same time increase their potassium intake, particularly by eating more fresh fruit and vegetables, they can keep all the problems of swelling to a minimum. Why not try it? You may be surprised at how effective this diet is. However, if you are on diuretics, do talk to your doctor before cutting back on your sodium intake.

Remember that another important factor in the retention of sodium and water is varying your eating, particularly changing your sodium and carbohydrate intake. Many people try to lose weight by crash dieting. Often, they fast effectively for several days and then go out and have a large meal. This causes great retention of sodium and therefore water, so that they swell up. If you want to lose weight, it is much more sensible to reduce food intake over a long period and get used to eating less food. It is important to take regular meals rather than trying a crash diet followed by binging.

Sodium and heart failure

The heart pumps the blood around the body. Sometimes, if the arteries are narrowed and this has caused damage to the muscle of the heart, then it is not able to pump properly. When this happens, the kidney retains more sodium and water to try and help the heart pump better; but this fluid retention unfortunately often makes the heart pump less well. Diuretics are given to get rid of the extra sodium and water. Another way is to restrict the amount of sodium in the diet, sometimes along with, and sometimes instead of taking the pills. Many studies have shown that this can be very helpful.

If you have heart failure and feel that you would like to try cutting down on sodium, you must discuss it with your doctor. The combination of a very low sodium diet and diuretics can occasionally be dangerous as the amount of sodium in the blood may be reduced too much. Many people who do cut back on their sodium intake will find that they will not need to take the diuretic they are on or, at the very least, will be able to reduce the dose, but you do need proper medical advice about this.

Sodium and liver disease

When the liver is damaged, the kidney may retain sodium and water, leading to swelling, and so again cutting back on sodium intake in the diet can be of great help. As with heart failure, it is very important if you have liver disease to discuss this first with your doctor. It may well be necessary to adjust your dose of diuretics.

Sodium and kidney disease

The kidney is an extremely important organ that not only controls the amount of sodium in the body but also gets rid of impurities from the blood. In some illnesses where the kidney stops working properly, its ability to get rid of sodium is reduced, often causing high blood pressure. Reducing sodium intake can be helpful in reducing the blood pressure. However, if the kidney is badly affected, a severe reduction in sodium intake may impair the working of the kidney further.

In another form of kidney disease, where protein is lost in the urine, the so-called 'nephrotic syndrome', there is retention by the kidney of sodium and water, often with very great swelling. Diuretics are nearly always needed to control the swelling, but reduction in sodium intake can be very helpful. This often means that a lower dose of the diuretics can be taken.

In some very rare forms of kidney disease the kidney is unable to hold on to sodium and there is a loss of it from the body, and so it may be dangerous to cut back on sodium intake. It is vital if you have kidney disease to discuss with your doctor whether it is a good idea for you to reduce your salt intake.

Should we all cut back on sodium intake?

Of all the conditions I have described, high blood pressure is most commonly linked to the high-sodium diet. Experts are divided as to whether this high-sodium diet we eat in the West is a problem only to those susceptible to high blood pressure or whether we are all making our blood pressures slightly higher. Tests on animals suggest that cutting back on sodium intake over a generation would lower everyone's blood pressure rather than just those who have high blood pressure. If it did, it would reduce the chances of stroke and heart attacks, therefore improving the general health of the whole population. The animal studies show that it is very important that sodium intake should be restricted from the first years of life. We do know that even if your pressure is in the normal range but at the higher end your chances of reaching the high blood pressure area as you grow older are greater (see the diagram on page 17).

Decisions on public health have often been taken as a result of educated guesses in the face of an epidemic although there was no proof of the cause. For example, vaccination for smallpox, and the provision of clean water and drainage at the time of the typhoid and cholera epidemics in Europe in the nineteenth century were introduced in these circumstances. Some of these changes were opposed by the medical profession at the time and evidence that they were beneficial came only after they were made. It looks as if there will be the same pattern in preventing high blood pressure. Many countries are now recommending a general reduction in sodium intake for the whole community rather than just for those with high blood pressure. Not all doctors agree with this policy and only time will tell whether it is correct. Nevertheless, if it does mean lower blood pressure in the whole community, there will be a substantial benefit. There is, in any case, a general consensus amongst nutritional experts that a more healthful diet should be eaten and that one aspect of this more healthful diet is to reduce the amount of sodium or salt in the diet. Remember that cutting salt intake moderately is unlikely to be harmful and food without the addition of large amounts of chemicals tastes better.

Are there any dangers to reducing sodium intake?

If you stick rigidly to the diet suggested in this book, you will be eating approximately 25 mmol (600 mg) of sodium per day. If you stick to it less rigidly your sodium intake will be around 60 to 80 mmol (1500 mg) per day. That is probably half of what you are now eating. Nevertheless, these amounts are three to ten times the quantities eaten by humans over the last million years and still eaten in many communities in, the world at the present time. There will be a slight reduction in the fluid bathing the tissues, about 5 per cent, but this will not normally make any difference.

However, there are two conditions where it could have an effect: first, in Addison's disease, when the adrenal gland (situated above the kidneys) fails. The adrenal gland secretes hormones that regulate the amount of sodium in the body. When the gland fails, the body loses sodium, which can cause a loss of fluid around the body cells. Second, in some forms of kidney disease the kidney is not able to hold on to sodium (see page 19). If there's any chance of you having either condition, or if you are in any doubt, do consult your doctor before reducing your sodium intake.

Other situations where a note of caution should be sounded are:

1. If you take vigorous physical exercise, particularly if you sweat a lot.
2. If you suddenly go from a cold environment to a very hot climate.

In these two cases it is important that sodium intake is reduced over a period, say a couple of weeks. On a high-salt intake, the sweat contains large amounts of sodium whereas on a low-salt intake, it will contain much less, in fact virtually none. This reduction in the amount of sodium in the sweat takes time and a sudden reduction by somebody who is losing large amounts of sweat may be dangerous as the body will continue to lose sodium in the sweat before the compensatory mechanisms come in to adjust it to a lower level. Once you have adjusted to the lower level there is no danger except under the most extreme conditions. Venezuelan Indians living in a very hot and humid climate survive on fifty times less sodium than the diet that we are recommending.

Measuring salt or sodium intake

The average salt intake at the present time in the West is around 8 to 12 g per day, that is, about two teaspoonfuls. The aim is to reduce this by at least half. When measuring the salt (sodium chloride) intake, it is the sodium content that we are concerned with. The sodium intake is usually measured in millimoles, i.e., one-thousandth of a mole (a scientific unit of measurement for comparing different substances); The measurement can also be expressed in grams. When sodium levels are expressed in mmol, we can make comparisons with amounts of other molecules in the body. The conversion of grams to these Standard International Units is:

1 g of sodium chloride = 17.1 mmol of sodium
1 g of sodium = 43.5 mmol of sodium
1 g of potassium chloride = 13.4 mmol of potassium
1 g of potassium = 25.6 mmol of potassium

Note: 1 gram = 1000 milligrams

If the average sodium intake is 8 to 12 g per day, this will come out in mmols of sodium as 136 to 205 mmol per day. As this is a more modern way of measuring sodium, we have used mmols throughout the book, but in the recipes you will find the equivalent amount in milligrams (one-thousandth of a gram) of sodium as well. It does not really matter if you do not understand exactly what a mmol means as all that is important is knowing that the total amount on a normal Western diet ranges from 120 to 250 mmol per day and on a very low sodium diet it is around 10 mmol per day and what we are aiming for is to reduce sodium intake to between 60 to 80 mmol per day.

By calculating from the tables on pages 99–105 and the recipes the amount of sodium in the different foods that you eat, you can come up roughly with the amount of sodium that you are eating per day.

The most accurate way of measuring sodium intake is to record the amount coming out in the urine. This is not something you can do at home, nor is it necessary, but if you are being tested at a hospital, this is how it will be done.

How do you go about reducing sodium intake?

Assuming you have been recommended by your doctor to reduce your sodium intake because of a medical condition, or perhaps you are quite fit and healthy but believe, like us, that reducing the amount of salt we eat can certainly do no harm, and will probably do a lot of good in the long run, you will wonder how to achieve this drastic cut of one half. Surprisingly, it is remarkably easy and once you have become used to it, the food will taste very much better as you begin to notice and enjoy the subtler, more varied flavors of less salty foods. There are four important simple steps:

1. Remove the salt shaker from the table. This is no hardship; 10 to 50 per cent of your salt intake comes from salt added at the table, yet studies done in Australia showed that when the hole in the salt shaker was half the normal size, people added half the quantity of salt to their food.

2. Stop adding salt to cooking, or reduce it by half. To begin with, food that you cook will taste rather bland but allow your taste receptors to adjust over a few weeks.

3. Avoid high-sodium foods, 'containing any form of sodium, including salt – usually these are processed foods. By using more natural foods such as fresh meat, fish, fruit and vegetables, you will immediately be on a fairly low-sodium diet.

    Some processed foods are allowed, depending on their sodium content (see detailed table of foods, page 99).

4. Look at the recipe section in this book for ideas on making food really appetizing. Remember, you can use your own recipes as well as long as you do not use table salt or any of the other sodium salts in them, and avoid the high-salt processed foods (beware of misleadingly labelled 'low-sodium' salts; for more on this, see page 27).

What problems are there on a low-sodium diet?

The initial bland taste of food   The salty taste of food is sensed by receptors on the tongue and mouth. The sensitivity of these receptors is reduced by increasing the amount of salt in the diet. On the high-salt diet that is at present eaten in the West, these receptors need very large amounts of sodium to notice a salty taste. However, once you have adjusted to a low-sodium diet, very small amounts of sodium produce a better salty taste. This adjustment in the salt-taste receptors does take time, anything from two to six weeks. Do not be surprised when you reduce your salt intake that food will start by tasting bland. Allow your taste receptors to adjust. When people stop adding large amounts of sugar to tea or coffee, similarly they find it difficult, but once adjusted, they realize that there are a lot of subtle flavors to different coffees and teas that they never appreciated before.

Natural foods have their own subtle flavors and can be varied by using flavors other than salt (see page 30). On a low-salt diet you will find that you become very much more discerning in distinguishing between different foods.

High-salt foods become unpleasant   Once adjusted to a low-sodium diet, you will find some of the very high salt foods you used to eat unpleasant. Many of our patients complain that these foods taste as though they have a chemical added which, of course, they have – salt is just a chemical. The problem arises when you are offered nothing but salty foods, perhaps salted nuts and chips at a party or a salty meal at a friend's house.

The problem of processed foods   Most processed and prepared convenience foods have had sodium added in quite large amounts. Sticking to a low-sodium diet will mean giving up these particular foods. This can be difficult for people who don't have much time to prepare food and want to use convenience foods. Even worse in this respect are snack foods; it is almost impossible outside health food shops to buy snack foods that have not had very large amounts of sodium added to them.

Eating out in restaurants   If you have been recommended a low-salt diet or have decided yourself to stick rigidly to one, you must choose your restaurant carefully. You are less able to control the salt content of your food than at home. As fast and convenience foods generally contain very large amounts of sodium – a well-known brand of hamburger and French fries contains almost 100 mmol (6 g) of sodium, as does a well-known brand of fried chicken – avoid fast-food eating places. Much Chinese and Japanese food has large amounts of sodium added, not only as salt but also as monosodium glutamate, so you will have to forego this sort of food too. Even in restaurants offering freshly cooked foods, the sodium content will depend first on the type of food and second on the chef. But here you should be able to select foods that are lower in sodium and some hotels and restaurants now promote the fact that they will prepare low-sodium foods. Some restaurants cook dishes to order, such as omelettes, hamburgers, broiled steaks and fish, kabobs and tandoori chicken, in which case you can request these without added salt. Again, the more pressure that is brought to bear, the quicker restaurants and hotels will begin to cater for people who wish to cut back on their salt intake.

With friends   You will have to be tactful. With people you know well and who do their own cooking, it is a good idea to say beforehand that you are now on a low-salt diet, and give them some idea of the type of food you can eat. It is not worth ruining friendships by offending, though. If you think asking for special food might do this, be prepared to eat just one high-salt meal. A very occasional lapse shouldn't hurt you.

Salt in our present diet

We can get a better understanding of how to restrict sodium intake in the diet by looking at exactly how the sodium content of our present diet is made up.

Added salt   Ten to 40 per cent of salt intake is added either at the table or in the cooking. It is important to remember that salt is not only present in table salt, but in all other forms – Kosher salt, rock salt, sea salt, herb salt, garlic salt, and in other flavorings such as monosodium glutamate and tomato paste.

Processed food   Processed food usually contains large amounts of sodium and can make up anything from 20 to 70 per cent of sodium intake. Sodium is added to processed food for several reasons:

● Flavor: the processing of food often removes the natural taste. In order to restore it, sodium chloride and monosodium glutamate are added as flavor enhancers. (The table below shows all the sodium compounds used in processed foods.) There has been a tendency over the last few years to increase the amount of sodium in these foods. Whether it is necessary to add so much sodium is a matter of debate. Perhaps it is due to the fact that the food tasters employed by the food industry have a very high sodium intake and a suppressed salt taste threshold. If this were so, they would need very large amounts of sodium in the food they were tasting before a salty taste were to be appreciated. Another factor that may be important is that salty foods make you thirsty so you drink more which is, presumably, good for the drink industry.

   The food manufacturers claim that if they reduce the amount of sodium, there may be wholesale rejection of some of their processed foods. There is no evidence for this but the manufacturers are unlikely to change unless there is considerable public pressure. However, most companies are very ethical and will change if they feel that there is a consensus of opinion that their foods should contain less sodium. In many countries in the West, food

Sodium compounds used in processed foods

Compound	Purpose
Salt/sodium chloride	Flavor enhancer, preservative
Sodium bicarbonate	Used in self-rising flour*
Sodium nitrite	A preservative and also used to improve coloring in cured meats
Monosodium glutamate	Flavor enhancer
Sodium saccharin	A sweetener†
Sodium benzoate	Preservative in sauces, relishes and salad dressings
Sodium alginate	An emulsifier used in ice cream and drinks
Sodium sulphite	Preservative in some dried fruits

*Remember it is possible to use potassium bicarbonate, see page 34
† The amount is usually trivial in terms of total sodium intake.

manufacturers are now producing a range of low-sodium products.

• Preservative: sodium chloride is the oldest preservative known, but its preservative role is nowadays very limited, with the introduction of other preservatives and particularly since the development of the refrigerator and deep-freeze; although salt is still used in smoked fish and meat such as ham and bacon, in cheese and butter and in pickles. In all of these it may be possible to substitute potassium for the sodium. At present, however, potassium is not widely used and so it is a more expensive preservative.

• Part of the food processing: sodium is commonly used to form a gel with the meat and fat in canned meats. It acts as a binding agent, retaining water, therefore making the product heavier and, according to food manufacturers, more acceptable to the customer!
Sodium is also used to develop the full color of products, particularly of ham, bacon and sausages.
At one time salt was used to stop the growth of wild yeast and promote the fermentation of bread dough.

• Labelling of foods with sodium content: more progressive food manufacturers in some countries are labelling their foods with the approximate sodium content. Usually, this is the approximate sodium content per average serving. Some manufacturers are opposed to or are resisting the labelling of the sodium content of foods. Yet, if foods were properly labelled with their sodium content, it would be possible for people who wished to stick to a low-sodium diet to buy a lot more processed food – anything with a sufficiently low-sodium content.

Other sources of sodium

Some medicines contain sodium and often pills are made up of sodium salts. However, the amount of sodium contained in these is usually very little.
One important source of sodium is some of the antacids. Sodium bicarbonate has the highest content of all, but should not in any case be used as an antacid. Another is the various liver salts, or health or fruit salts. Indeed, any effervescent medicine is likely to contain sodium bicarbonate. To check which others contain a lot of sodium, look at the bottle or ask your pharmacist.

Water and soft drinks   The sodium content of drinking water varies quite widely. In general it is not an important source of sodium as most people drink only one to two liters (four to eight glasses) of water a day. For example, water after treatment ranges from 6 mg of sodium per liter to 50 mg of sodium per liter, depending on the reservoir and source of water. In a few areas of the world the sodium content of water is much higher and can contribute to the total sodium intake in the diet, particularly if you are on a low-sodium diet. But in 99 per cent of cases there is no need to take drinking water into account.

Some mineral waters do contain very high amounts of sodium and you can certainly taste the salt; Vichy water contains approximately 70 mmol per liter (1600 mg per liter). Most others are low in sodium and can be safely drunk. The quantity is usually given on the label.

In soft drinks the sodium composition varies depending on the source of water that they are made with. On the whole, they are not an important source of sodium.

Water softeners   These are used to make soap lather more effectively. They work by adding sodium to the water to get rid of the hardening mineral, calcium. The amount of sodium added is not very large and drinking softened water will not increase sodium intake significantly. But there are other reasons for not drinking softened water. First, it is more likely to absorb metals from the pipes, particularly lead (though lead pipes are not common now), and second, there is evidence that the number of heart attacks in a community is directly related to the degree of softness of water – the harder the water, the fewer heart attacks. It is generally recommended that a tap with hard water should be left for drinking purposes if you have a water softener.

Salt substitutes

Reading about all the categories of foods that contain sodium, you may think you will have some trouble producing an appetizing, salt-free diet. There are plenty of ways of doing this, as we show in the next section, How to Cook Without Salt. First I would like to explain the benefits and disadvantages of salt substitutes.

Mineral salt is a mixture of sodium and potassium, sometimes with the addition of a small amount of magnesium. People using substitutes say this is more acceptable than a pure potassium substitute as it does not have such a bitter aftertaste. But it still contains large amounts of sodium. A study done in Finland showed that people who used mineral salt consumed more of it than of sodium chloride as they thought the mineral salt was good for them, and so they did not after all reduce their sodium intake.

You will need to read the labels carefully. If a mineral salt contains sodium chloride, do not use it. Remember, if you have kidney disease never use a salt substitute without consulting your doctor.

Salt substitutes containing potassium chloride rather than

sodium chloride have been around for many years and may be helpful for anyone who is in the habit of adding salt to food and finds it very difficult to give it up. However, our experience is that many people find these salt substitutes have a rather bitter after-taste. If you want to try one, start with a very small amount added to the cooking or at the table. Make sure that it contains no sodium.

Potassium

Potassium is a vital constituent of our diet. It is present in the body mainly inside cells (see page 10). There is evidence in both animals and humans that not only a high-salt but also a low-potassium intake is likely to raise blood pressure. In addition we now have some evidence that increasing potassium intake does lower blood pressure, and it is interesting that vegetarians, who in general have a higher potassium intake than non-vegetarians, usually have lower blood pressure. An increase in potassium intake helps get rid of sodium through the kidney and it is probably this effect that lowers blood pressure, although a lot more work is needed before we can be certain.

Unlike sodium, potassium is present in large quantities in fruit and vegetables, meat and fish, and during evolution and in some primitive tribes today, large amounts of potassium were eaten – around 100 to 200 mmol (4 to 8 g) per day. As we eat less fruit and vegetables and more processed food in the West, potassium intake has fallen on the average to around 30 to 80 mmols (1 to 3 g) per day.

At the present time it would seem sensible to increase potassium intake, particularly by eating more fresh fruit and vegetables. Their taste, very lightly cooked or raw, is good without any added salt; the combination of onion, carrot and celery provides a superb flavor and is the basis for many stocks and stews.

There is a possible danger in increasing potassium intake for people with kidney disease. The kidney may have problems in getting rid of high levels of potassium, which may lead to a rise in the level of potassium in the blood. This could cause severe problems with the heart. If you have problems with the kidney, heart or liver, do not increase potassium intake or use a potassium salt substitute before consulting your doctor.

Other ways of eating healthily

Reducing your sodium intake is one of the most important factors in making the diet more healthy. If you are interested in eating a healthy diet it makes sense to combine the low-salt approach with other changes recommended by nutritional experts that will help control obesity, prevent the development of arterial disease and reduce the risk of heart disease.

Eat less fat   On the average, people in Western countries need to reduce fat intake by one-third. Remember that fat is a very large source of calories and eating a high-fat diet is usually responsible for people being overweight. At the same time, it is thought that saturated fat can put up your blood cholesterol.

To cut fat consumption, do not fry food but broil it. Cut all visible fat off meat; remember that even lean red meat contains large amounts of fat. Foods containing their own fat need nothing added for broiling; they can also be fried in a heavy nonstick skillet without fat, and this way lose quite a lot of extra fat. Eat more fish and white meat.

Cut down on milk, cheese, butter and margarine. If you try skim milk, remember that although it contains less fat than full milk it is quite a high sodium-containing food.

Many experts feel that as well as reducing total fat intake, some of the polyunsaturated fats should be substituted for saturated fats. Use cooking oils that are labelled high in polyunsaturates, usually corn oil, soybean oil and sunflower oil. Many cheaper blended vegetable oils are high in saturated fat.

Eat less sugar   Sugar is second to fat as a source of calories. Too many calories mean that you will get fat. Try to cut back on candies, chocolates and soft drinks. A high sugar intake also increases the chances of diabetes developing and is the prime cause of tooth decay. Most people need to reduce the amount of sugar they eat by half.

Eat more fiber   Fiber is the name given to a range of complex plant substances that pass through the intestine and are not absorbed. By providing roughage, they aid digestion and help prevent constipation. There is some evidence that they may reduce blood cholesterol and blood sugar as well as a suggestion that they may even lower blood pressure. Fiber is mainly present in wholewheat flour and bread, wholegrain cereals, pasta and rice and in fresh vegetables and fruit.

Fruit and vegetables   Try to eat more fresh fruit and vegetables. This means that you will be eating less fat, more fiber and potassium, at the same time as eating very little sodium. If you can't always buy fresh, the best substitute is frozen, not dried or canned, which have less nutritional value and often salt added in the latter.

In developing the recipes and making recommendations in this book we have always followed the above advice.

HOW TO COOK WITHOUT SALT

Here are some guidelines on cooking for a salt-free diet. Cutting out salt and salty foods and substituting new flavors soon become second nature, and introduce variety into your eating. The table opposite outlines the broad groups of foods with high and low-salt content.

1. Do not use any form of Kosher or table salt, or other forms of salt such as sea salt, garlic salt or celery salt. Remember that flavor enhancers nearly always contain sodium, particularly in the form of monosodium glutamate. Do not use mineral salt, which contains a mixture of potassium and sodium salts and is not suitable for a restricted sodium diet. However, you may use a potassium salt substitute. Make sure that it is one that does not contain sodium and use it very sparingly as you may find that it has a bitter aftertaste, particularly when you first use it.

2. Replace salt with various spices, such as freshly ground pepper, paprika, cayenne pepper, chili powder (use this sparingly at first; you may find its flavor very powerful), ginger, fresh or ground, cinnamon, curry powder, garam masala, nutmeg and cloves.

3. Make your own salt-free stock. It can be stored and will always come in useful (page 45).

4. For varied flavors try dry mustard, lemon juice, vinegar, white or red wine, cider or beer.

5. Use plenty of onions, shallots, garlic, fresh chili peppers (use with care as some are very hot). All of these are particularly good added to stews.

6. Fresh herbs, such as parsley, chives, mint, thyme, sage, rosemary, basil and tarragon are all excellent to flavor a salt-free dish. They can be grown in pots on a sunny windowsill, and can be bought from any good garden center or grown from seeds. Fresh herbs can be frozen or dried.

7. If fresh herbs are not available, they can be replaced with dried herbs. Mixed dried herbs are excellent and easy to use.

    Most of the recipes use dried herbs for convenience, but try using fresh herbs if you have some and adjust the quantity according to your taste. In general, you will need slightly more of the fresh herbs than the equivalent dried.

Guide to sodium content

Foods with a low-sodium content (eat freely)
Vegetables: all kinds except canned or dried
Fruit: all kinds, fresh, frozen, dried or canned
Meat, fish, eggs, poultry (not commercially prepared)
Salt-free butter, salt-free margarine, fresh cream
Salt-free bread, pasta and rice
Unsalted nuts
Fruit juices, soft drinks
Tea, coffee
Sugar, jam, marmalade, honey, hard candy, peppermints

Foods with a medium-sodium content (limit or avoid)
Canned vegetables
Milk, yogurt and milk puddings
Salted butter and margarine
Purchased bread, cakes, cookies, pastry
Breakfast cereals
Bottled sauces and ketchups
Chocolate

Foods with a high-sodium content (do not eat)
Table salt
Bacon, ham, cured meat, canned meat, salami, sausages, purchased pâté
Smoked fish, canned fish
Cheese
Canned and packaged soups
Bouillon cubes, yeast and meat extracts
Vegetable juices, soy sauce

For more detailed information on the sodium content of various foods see pages 99–105.

Vegetables
● Use plenty of fresh vegetables and salads. You will see in the table of sodium contents of vegetables that some contain slightly more sodium than others, but not so much that they should be avoided.

● Frozen vegetables can usually be eaten as most have no sodium added (check the label). Remember though that prepared vegetables with a sauce have had sodium added.

● When cleaning vegetables, never use salt or baking soda.

● Do not add any salt when cooking.

● It is a good idea to try to retain the potassium when cooking vegetables. Do not boil but steam them. Put the vegetables in an ordinary pan, add a small quantity of unsalted water, approximately 120 ml/½ cup per 450 g/1 lb of vegetable. Cover the pan and cook over very low heat until just tender and still crisp. Alternatively, you can cook vegetables over a pan of simmering water in a colander. It is not really necessary to have a special steamer.

● If a sauce is required for the vegetables, for example, cauliflower or spinach, or gravy for meat, use the normal amount of boiling water and retain the liquid left from the cooking, which is salt-free, has a good flavor and is rich in potassium.

If you are not using the cooking liquid this way, keep it and use it later as stock either for soup or a stew.

● Avoid any canned or dried vegetables except canned tomatoes, which do not usually contain any salt (check the label) and cans labelled 'no salt added'. Do not use instant potato or tomato juice. Salt-free tomato paste can be obtained; look at the label. If you are not able to find it, use a small amount of the ordinary type. This will not contribute too much salt to your intake.

● Legumes (dried beans, peas and lentils) are low in sodium and fat, high in fiber and make a good and economical substitute for meat as they contain protein. Soaking and cooking times depend on the type, and the package will give instructions. Always soak and cook legumes in salt-free water. It is very important that they are boiled for at least 10 minutes at the beginning of the cooking time as some beans can cause acute vomiting and diarrhea if not boiled.

Fruit
● You can eat any kind of fruit: fresh, frozen, canned or dried. If you eat canned fruit try to choose those in their natural juice without large amounts of added sugar. Remember that if you eat the skin of the fruit you will also be eating more fiber.

Meat and poultry
● You can eat any kind of lean beef, pork, lamb, rabbit, liver, kidney or poultry, whether fresh or frozen. Remember, however, that frozen prepared meat dishes will have salt added.

Do not eat any kind of commercially prepared meat products such as sausages, canned meat, hamburgers, pâté, meat pies or meat spreads. You can make your own hamburgers and pâté free of added salt (see pages 50, 72).

● When cooking meat or poultry, never add salt. Flavor it instead with fresh or dried herbs such as rosemary or mint for lamb, thyme or sage for pork, black pepper and mixed herbs for beef, tarragon, sage or thyme for chicken – or any other herbs you may like to try. You can also rub the skin of the meat with dry mustard, but remember that prepared mustards have salt added so do not use these. If you like the flavor of garlic, try making small cuts in a roast and filling them with garlic slivers before roasting.

● Avoid frying meat. Broil or cook in the oven whenever you can. If you do fry it, use a minimum of oil and a nonstick pan. A lot of meat can even be fried without any added fat, as a sufficient amount will be released during cooking.

●   You must avoid any kind of smoked meat, for instance, bacon and ham, as these have had large amounts of sodium chloride and other sodium salts added to them. If, occasionally, you wish to eat a slice of bacon, or to cook a ham perhaps for Christmas, you can reduce the salt content by soaking the meat in water for at least a day or, in the case of sliced bacon, for a few hours. Change the water two or three times during soaking, then drain the meat and wash it under a cold tap. If you are cooking a ham, you can boil it for half the cooking time and change the water once during cooking. Finish cooking the ham by baking it in the oven. Even with all this preparation, ham will still contain large amounts of salt so do not eat too much – try to avoid it if you can!

Fish
●   You can eat as much fresh or frozen fish as you like. It may be baked or broiled. If you fry fish, use a minimum of oil.

●   You must avoid smoked fish and all commercially prepared fish such as fish sticks, fish cakes, canned fish and frozen fish that is prepared in sauce and bread crumbs. All of these have had salt added to them.

Shellfish
●   All shellfish are unfortunately high in sodium and should be avoided if possible. However, small amounts are not absolutely forbidden! Remember that you can reduce the sodium content by boiling them in salt-free water.

Commercially prepared shrimp often have a glaze added to them which has sodium in it.

Dairy foods
●   Unsalted butter is available in many supermarkets, but it is preferable to use salt-free polyunsaturated margarine which can be bought in most health food shops.

It is much better to broil food, but if you must fry it, use polyunsaturated vegetable oils such as corn, sunflower, safflower or soybean.

●   All cheese contains salt. If you must include it in your cooking, use it very sparingly and choose a cheese with a low-sodium content, such as mild cheddar, parmesan, cottage cheese or mozzarella cheese. Grating the cheese makes it go further in many dishes.

Cream cheese is quite low in sodium, but use it only occasionally as it has a very high fat content.

●   Low-fat yogurt may be used in small quantities.

●   Fresh cream, while high in fats and not recommended for that reason, may be eaten on special occasions.

• Milk contains quite large quantities of sodium so use only small amounts. Skim milk has the same sodium content as whole milk but contains less fat and so is preferable from that point of view.

• Eggs may be eaten as a main course instead of meat or fish, but don't forget that the yolks are very high in cholesterol, so use whole eggs sparingly.

Bread, cakes and cereals

• Try to cook with plain wholewheat flour. Plain white flour can be used in some recipes or mixed with wholewheat flour. Do not use self-rising flour, ordinary baking powder or baking soda, as they all contain sodium. You can buy baking powder substitute which is salt-free and contains potassium. This is available from some health food shops, or you can ask your local pharmacy to make it up (see page 97). You can make your own self-rising flour by mixing plain flour with the potassium baking powder substitute.

• Bread that you buy in the shops is a high-salt food. Some health food shops have salt-free bread but it is generally hard to find. You may be able to persuade your local baker to cook a batch of salt-free bread for you, and you can then freeze it. Why not instead try making your own salt-free wholewheat or white bread using the recipes in this book.

• Remember that all manufactured crackers, cookies, cakes and crisp breads contain salt or sodium so make your own using the recipes in this book. If your favorite cake or cookie recipe is not amongst them, use your recipe but replace the ordinary margarine or butter with all-purpose polyunsaturated salt-free margarine or salt-free butter and the self-rising flour with flour and a baking powder substitute.
All cakes and cookies contain fairly large amounts of fat so try to keep them for special occasions only.

• Most breakfast cereals contain quite large amounts of salt; you must avoid these. Those that are low in sodium are Puffed Wheat, Shredded Wheat, Sugar Puffs and rolled oats.

• You can eat any kind of pasta, preferably wholewheat, or rice, again preferably brown unpolished or wild rice. Remember to cook these in unsalted water.

• Other cereals such as wheat, oats, rye, barley, corn and buck-wheat are all salt-free and can be used.

Sauces

• Do not use any manufactured sauces, for example, tomato catsup, salad dressing, Worcestershire sauce, soy sauce, mayon-naise, horseradish or prepared mustards unless labelled salt-free. Some health food shops stock a range of sauces which are low in sodium, and you can make your own salt-free tomato sauce or mayonnaise using our recipes.

• Avoid using bouillon cubes, gravy powders and concentrated vegetable, yeast or meat extracts as they are all very high in sodium. Make your own salt-free stock using our recipe.

Drinks
• Tea, coffee, most carbonated drinks such as cola and fruit juices, are low in sodium. Club soda, one or two mineral waters, and some other carbonated glucose drinks, have some sodium in them (see page 27).

• Alcoholic beverages can be taken in moderation: 1–2 glasses of wine or of beer or 1 or 2 measures of liquor per day maximum (the sodium contents of the different alcoholic beverages are listed on page 105). Remember that excessive alcohol intake causes damage to the liver and other vital organs. It is also associated with high blood pressure.

• Milk and skim milk are high in sodium (see above) and should be used only sparingly as an additive to tea or coffee.

Packed lunches
• These represent quite a problem as the conventional sandwich lunch has a high-sodium content. Reduce this by making sandwiches with salt-free, preferably wholewheat bread (see recipe page 94) and use polyunsaturated salt-free margarine or unsalted butter.

• Fill the sandwiches with a selection of lettuce, cucumber, tomato, celery, carrot, watercress and onion combined with homemade salt-free mayonnaise or dressing;

or

salt-free pâté (see page 50) or your own cold, cooked meat, for example, beef, pork, lamb, chicken or turkey – do not use ham, sausage or salami, canned meat, commercially prepared pâté or meat spreads;

or

you can occasionally use eggs, a little cottage or cream cheese, or a small slice of mild cheddar cheese but remember the warnings about fat and cholesterol in dairy products;

or

try sweet fillings such as mashed banana, chopped dates or a little cream cheese mixed with nuts and raisins or chopped pineapple.

• You could sometimes include a homemade salt-free quiche or turnover filled with meat or vegetables. 'Sausage' rolls can be made salt-free with a spiced ground meat mixture instead of the sausage. Any pastry has a high-fat content so these should be taken only occasionally, for variety.

● You can eat any fresh salad with your own salt-free dressing, but do not buy commercially prepared salads.

● Fresh fruit is a perfect ending to any meal. Always try to include it. Mixed salt-free nuts and raisins, homemade cakes, cookies or fruit pie are alternatives, but try to keep the baked foods for special occasions as they are high in fat and calories.

Availability of low-sodium or salt-free products

With the increasing publicity about the dangers of salt, many food manufacturers are now producing low-sodium or no-salt-added products. Some are obtainable in supermarkets and others are available only through health food shops. Many of these products are suitable for people on a low-salt diet, but you will need to read the labels very carefully. They cannot be listed individually due to wide variations from one country to another and the fact that they are coming out in increasing numbers every few months. They can be broadly categorized into:

1. **Dairy products** eg, low-sodium butter, low-sodium margarine (preferably labelled 'high in polyunsaturates') and in some countries, low-sodium cheeses.

2. **Cereal products** eg, low-sodium bread and crackers. It is important to ask how much sodium is in bread; try to obtain bread with none added.

3. **Canned products**, either low-sodium or no-salt-added eg, vegetables, soups, meats.

4. **Low-sodium sauces** eg, tomato catsup, mayonnaise, mustard.

5. **Low-sodium dried products**, eg, dried soups.

It is likely that there will be an increasing range of all these products, including frozen prepared meals. The greater the demand, the greater will be the availability of these products.

Don't forget the four steps in the salt-free diet:

1. Remember that initally the food will taste bland.
2. Allow time for your taste receptors to adjust, probably around two weeks.
3. You will then find you will be able to detect sodium in food very

easily. Your new diet will taste much better and you will be able to distinguish between different foods very much more easily.

4. Salted food and salt will taste unpleasant like a chemical. It is!

THE RECIPES

Weights and measures

The sodium and potassium content per serving for each recipe are shown in millimoles (mmol) and milligrams (mg). For simplicity, in the table on pages 99–105, giving both the sodium and potassium content of individual foods, they are only given in mmol. If you want to convert the mmol figure to mg, multiply by 23 for sodium and 39 for potassium. If you wish to convert mg into grams of sodium, divide by 1000. If you want to convert the sodium content of a meal in grams to its equivalent in sodium chloride (salt), you should multiply by 2.5.

In the recipes and tables the figures have been approximated to the nearest whole number. Figures coming out at less than 1 mmol are considered negligible and listed Tr (trace) in the table.

One level teaspoon of salt contains 120 mmol of sodium and one level tablespoon of salt contains 360 mmol of sodium. The average sodium intake in the West is approximately between 120–250 mmol per day. If you stick to the diet outlined in this book, you will reduce your sodium intake to around 20–80 mmol per day, depending on how strictly you keep away from processed foods. It is very important to remember that while sodium chloride (salt) is added to the food during cooking, or at the table and sometimes as a preservative and is the main source of sodium in our diets, we must also take into account other forms of sodium which are added: sodium bicarbonate, monosodium glutamate, as well as the sodium naturally occurring in foods.

All figures for calculation of the tables have been taken from USDA Home and Garden Bulletin No 233, *The Sodium Content of your Food 1981* (US Government Printing Office, Washington, DC 20402, 1981); Bowe's and Church's *Food Values of Portions Commonly Used* Pennington and Church (J. B. Lippincott Company, Philadelphia, 13th edn, 1980); Agriculture Handbook No 8–1 to 8–10 *Composition of Foods* (USDA Science and Education Administration, Washington, DC 20402 1978).

The energy value is given in kilocalories. Kilocalories are commonly known as calories.

The recipe ingredients are in both metric and lb/cup/spoon

measurements. Slight approximations have been made, so do not mix the two in any one recipe.

The spoon measurements used in the recipes throughout are level unless otherwise stated. One teaspoon (tsp) = 5 ml; 1 tablespoon (tbsp) = 15 ml. To ensure success, use standard measuring spoons.

Sample meal plan

If you follow this meal plan, using recipes in the book as well as salt-free fresh foods, you will have a well-balanced, healthful diet.

Choose one of the suggested dishes from each of the categories in the different meals, and vary ingredients often enough to provide interest in your diet.

Regulate your calorie intake according to your needs by checking the calorie values of the recipes and in the tables on pages 99–105.

Don't forget, all food must be cooked and prepared without salt.

Breakfast
Fruit juice (not tomato)
Grapefruit, fresh or canned
Prunes, stewed fruit

Unsalted cereal: Shredded Wheat, Puffed Wheat, Sugar Puffs or oatmeal with a small amount of milk
Boiled, poached, scrambled egg occasionally

Salt-free bread, unsalted butter or salt-free margarine
Jam, marmalade or honey

Tea or coffee

Note If ordinary bread, rolls or crackers are taken, refer to the table (page 102) and count them in your daily salt allowance.

Lunch or light meal
Salt-free bread or rolls filled with cold sliced plain roast meats, egg, homemade meat loaf or pâté (page 50), or salad
Homemade savory pastries or quiche (page 92) filled with unsalted ground meat or vegetables
Salt-free crackers and a little cream cheese, cucumber and tomato.
Homemade hamburgers in a salt-free roll (pages 72, 95) with salad
Eggs, scrambled, poached, boiled (or occasionally fried) with baked or broiled tomatoes
Mixed salad with salt-free meat, eggs, cooked unsalted beans or unsalted peanuts

Rice salad (page 57) with a selection of chopped vegetables, nuts

Fresh fruit, mixed salt-free nuts and raisins, homemade cake or cookies (pages 85–91) (made with salt-free baking powder)

Tea, coffee, fruit drinks, fruit juices

Dinner or main meal
Homemade soup without bouillon cubes (pages 45–7)
Homemade pâté with salt-free bread (pages 50, 94)
Grapefruit, fruit juice (not tomato)
Avocado with vinaigrette dressing or homemade mayonnaise (page 48)

Meat or fish, broiled, baked or roasted
Meat or vegetable casserole (pages 60, 74)
Homemade pie or turnover (page 80)
Nut or bean dish (page 59)

Vegetables or salad (use salt-free dressing)

Rice, pasta, potatoes or bread

Fresh or canned fruit
Gelatin dessert or small ice cream
Water ice (page 81)
Fruit pie or tart (pages 81–2)
Steamed or baked sponge cake made with salt-free baking powder
Baked apple

Heavy cream or small quantity of custard sauce

Tea, coffee

Note: If wine, beer or other alcoholic beverage is taken, check the amount of sodium it contains in the table (page 105).

A salt-free meal: French plum tart (*top*, see page 82), Chicken with rice and velouté sauce (*center left*, see page 79), Tossed green salad with curried dressing (*center right*, see page 56), Avocado with mayonnaise (*bottom*, see page 48).
OVERLEAF: Fish coquille (*left*, see page 51), Waldorf salad (*center*, see page 58), Country pâté (*bottom*, see page 50).

SOUPS

STOCKS

When making soups do not use bouillon cubes as they all contain salt. Instead make your own stock. The method is simple: place in a large pan any bones and roughly chopped vegetables, especially carrots, onions and celery. Add 1½–2 liters/quarts of water, flavor with your favorite herbs, one bay leaf and a few peppercorns, bring to a boil, reduce the heat and cover. Simmer for about 2 hours, then strain and allow to cool. Stock can be kept, covered, for about one week in a refrigerator or it can be frozen and used when required.

If you prefer to use a pure vegetable stock, omit the bones and add a few extra vegetables, such as leeks or turnips.

In all the soup recipes, water can be used instead of stock, but the flavor of the soup will, of course, not be as good as a soup made with homemade stock.

Garlic and tomato soup

Serves 4
Each serving: negligible sodium; 10 mmol (407 mg) potassium; 65 Kcal

15 ml/1 tbsp vegetable oil
450 g/1 lb tomatoes, chopped
2 onions, chopped
4 cloves garlic, finely chopped
5 ml/1 tsp dried thyme

1 bay leaf
25 g/4 tbsp all-purpose flour
freshly ground pepper
pinch chili powder
1 l/4½ cups water

Heat the oil in a pan. Add the tomatoes, onions, garlic, thyme and bay leaf and cook slowly for about 10 minutes, stirring occasionally. Stir in the flour. Pour in the water, bring to a boil, reduce the heat, add the pepper and chili powder, cover and simmer for 30 minutes. Remove the bay leaf and purée the soup in an electric blender or by rubbing through a sieve.

Return to the pan, reheat and serve hot.

Garlic and tomato soup (*top*), Split pea soup (*bottom*, see page 47).

Country vegetable soup

Serves 4
Each serving: 2 mmol (44 mg) sodium; 21 mmol (809 mg) potassium; 162 Kcal

15 ml/1 tbsp vegetable oil
2 medium-sized potatoes, peeled and chopped
2 leeks, sliced
l large onion, chopped
2 carrots, diced
2 celery leaves (optional)

50 g/¼ cup split peas (optional)
25 g/4 tbsp all-purpose flour
1 l/4½ cups homemade salt-free stock or water (do not use bouillon cubes)
freshly ground pepper
pinch chili powder

Heat the oil in a large pan. Add the vegetables and cook over moderate heat for 5–10 minutes, without browning them. Stir in the flour. Pour in the stock or water, bring to a boil, reduce the heat, season with pepper and chili powder, cover and simmer for about 20 minutes, until vegetables are tender.

If desired, purée in an electric blender or by rubbing through a sieve.

Return to the pan, reheat and serve hot.

Fish soup

Serves 4
Each serving: 3 mmol (77 mg) sodium; 12 mmol (492 mg) potassium; 113 Kcal

3 cloves
2 whole onions
225 g/1½ cups white fish, boned, skinned and chopped
2 carrots, diced
1 small leek, chopped
3 cloves garlic, finely chopped
1 l/4½ cups water

150 ml/½ cup white wine (optional)
freshly ground pepper
5 ml/1 tsp dried mixed herbs
5 ml/1 tsp ground fennel seeds (optional)
1 egg yolk
15 ml/1 tbsp lemon juice
pinch grated nutmeg

Stick the cloves into the onions. Put the fish in a large pan and add the onions, carrots, leek and garlic. Pour in 1 l/1¾ pints water and wine. Season with pepper, mixed herbs and fennel. Bring to a boil, reduce the heat, cover and simmer for 30 minutes. Purée in an electric blender or by rubbing through a sieve. Return to the pan. Mix together the egg yolk, lemon juice and nutmeg and stir into the soup. Reheat gently without boiling, stirring constantly.

Serve hot.

Curried vegetable soup

Serves 4
Each serving: negligible sodium; 12.3 mmol (479 mg) potassium; 61 Kcal

15 ml/1 tbsp vegetable oil
1 onion, sliced
2 cloves garlic, finely chopped
225 g/2 cups green beans, chopped
3 tomatoes, skinned and chopped

1 potato, diced
5 ml/1 tsp curry powder (or more to taste)
freshly ground pepper
1 l/4½ cups water

Heat the oil in a pan. Add the onion and garlic and cook gently. Stir in the beans, tomatoes, potato, curry powder and pepper. Pour in the water, bring to a boil, reduce the heat, cover and simmer for 35–40 minutes. Purée in an electric blender or by rubbing through a sieve.

Return to the pan and add more pepper or curry powder if necessary. Reheat and serve hot.

Split pea soup   See photograph, page 44

Serves 4
Each serving: 2 mmol (36 mg) sodium; 16 mmol (625 mg) potassium; 170 Kcal

225 g/1 cup split peas
1.3 l/6 cups water
1 carrot, diced
1 onion, finely chopped

2 sprigs parsley
1 small bay leaf
5 ml/1 tsp dried thyme
freshly ground pepper

Soak the split peas for one hour in cold water. Drain the peas, place in a saucepan, add the water and bring to a boil. Reduce the heat, skim the top, add the carrot, onion, parsley, bay leaf and thyme. Season with pepper, cover and cook for about 1½ hours. Purée in an electric blender or by rubbing through a sieve.

Return to the pan, reheat and serve hot, garnished with bread croûtons fried in a little vegetable oil and chopped parsley.

SAUCES, SNACKS AND APPETIZERS

Tomato sauce

Serves 4
Each serving: negligible sodium; 17 mmol (680 mg) potassium; 36 Kcal

900 g/2 lb ripe tomatoes, skinned
  and chopped
1 medium-sized onion, finely chopped
3 cloves garlic, finely chopped
1 bay leaf

10 ml/2 tsp dried mixed herbs or
  20 ml/1½ tbsp chopped mixed
  fresh herbs
freshly ground pepper

Plunge the tomatoes in boiling water for a few seconds, then skin them. Place the tomatoes, chopped onion and garlic in a pan. Add the bay leaf and herbs, season with pepper and simmer, uncovered, for about 1 hour. If the sauce becomes too dry, add a little water. Remove the bay leaf and serve hot.

If desired, the sauce can be puréed in an electric blender or by rubbing it through a sieve.

Variations   For a spicy tomato sauce add 2.5 ml/½ tsp chili powder.

If fresh tomatoes are unavailable, salt-free canned tomatoes can be used instead.

Mayonnaise

Serves 4–6
Each serving: negligible sodium; negligible potassium; 467–700 Kcal
Each level tablespoon (15 ml): negligible sodium; negligible potassium; 140 Kcal

2 egg yolks
300 ml/1¼ cups polyunsaturated
  vegetable oil
15 ml/1 tbsp white wine vinegar

freshly ground pepper

Garnish:
chopped chives or parsley

Place the egg yolks in a bowl and beat well. At first add the oil drop by drop, whisking continuously until the mayonnaise starts to thicken, then add the remaining oil in a slow stream, whisking all the time. Stir in the vinegar and pepper and garnish with chopped chives or parsley.

Crudités with garlic mayonnaise dip

Serves 6
Each serving: 4 mmol (105 mg) sodium; 17 mmol (654 mg) potassium; 116 Kcal

Garlic mayonnaise:
4 cloves garlic, crushed
2 egg yolks
300 ml/1¼ cups olive oil
15 ml/1 tbsp wine vinegar
freshly ground pepper

4 carrots, julienned
½ cauliflower, cut into florets
1 green pepper, cut into strips
1 red pepper, cut into strips
4 celery sticks, cut into equal lengths
12 scallions, trimmed

Crudités:
4 tomatoes, sliced or quartered
½ cucumber, cut into strips

Garnish:
chopped chives or chopped parsley

To make the garlic mayonnaise, mix together the crushed garlic and the egg yolks. Beat well. Add the oil, drop by drop whisking continuously until the mayonnaise starts to thicken, then add the remaining oil in a slow stream, whisking all the time. Stir in the vinegar and pepper.

Arrange the vegetables on a serving platter. Sprinkle the chopped chives or parsley over the garlic mayonnaise and serve separately.

Roasted peanuts

Each level tablespoon: negligible sodium; 2 mmol (82 mg) potassium; 71 Kcal

Use plain unsalted peanuts which can be obtained from health food and some other shops.

Preheat the oven to 350°F/180°C.

Place the peanuts on a baking sheet and bake for about 15 minutes, shaking the sheet occasionally. After baking, the skin of the peanuts will come away easily. Eat cold.

Variations Filberts and almonds can be roasted in the same way.

Hummus

Serves 2–3
Each serving: negligible sodium; 7–10 mmol (271–407 mg) potassium; 152–228 Kcal

100 g/½ cup chickpeas
4 cloves garlic, crushed
2.5 ml/½ tsp chili powder
freshly ground pepper
15 ml/1 tbsp olive oil

15 ml/1 tbsp wine vinegar

Garnish:
chopped parsley
paprika

Soak the chickpeas overnight in cold water. Drain, then cook them in plenty of unsalted water for 2–3 hours, or until tender. Drain, reserving about 200 ml/1 cup of the cooking liquid. Blend or mash the chickpeas and water until smooth and stir in the garlic, chili powder and pepper. Add the olive oil and vinegar, little by little, stirring all the time. The mixture should be smooth and fairly solid. Garnish with chopped parsley and paprika.

Serve with sliced raw vegetables and salt-free wholewheat or pita bread (pages 94, 96).

Variation   Add 15 ml/1 tbsp salt-free tahini (sesame seed paste) with the oil, lemon juice and parsley.

Leeks vinaigrette

Serves 4
Each serving: negligible sodium; 10 mmol (386 mg) potassium; 69 Kcal

*450 g/1 lb young leeks, trimmed
   and halved*

Dressing:
*45 ml/3 tbsp olive oil
15 ml/1 tbsp wine vinegar*

*1 small onion, finely chopped
1 clove garlic, crushed
freshly ground pepper*

Garnish:
chopped parsley

Place the leeks in a pan, add 120 ml/½ cup water, cover and cook over low heat for about 15 minutes. Drain the leeks and cool.

To make the vinaigrette, mix together the oil and vinegar, add the onion and garlic, and season with pepper.

Arrange the leeks on a serving dish, pour the vinaigrette over them and garnish with chopped parsley.

Country pâté   See photograph, page 43

Serves 6 to 8
Each serving: 4–5 mmol (89–119 mg) sodium; 6–8 mmol (386–580 mg) potassium; 298–397 Kcal

*450 g/1 lb fresh lean ground pork
350 g/¾ lb pork livers, ground
1 onion, finely chopped
2 cloves garlic, crushed
1 egg, beaten*

*10 ml/2 tsp dried mixed herbs
pinch cayenne pepper
15 ml/1 tbsp brandy
freshly ground pepper*

Preheat the oven to 325°F/160°C.

Mix together the ground pork, livers, onion, garlic, beaten egg, mixed herbs, cayenne pepper and brandy. Season with pepper.

Turn into a terrine or loaf pan and cover with foil. Bake for about 2 hours.

Cool in the pan before unmolding.

Fish coquille

See photograph, page 42

Serves 4

Each serving: 6 mmol (131 mg) sodium; 7 mmol (262 mg) potassium; 146 Kcal

45 ml/3 tbsp skim milk
2 egg yolks
50 g/½ cup grated low-salt cheese (mild cheddar, gouda, edam)
15 ml/1 tbsp lemon juice
15 ml/1 tbsp chopped parsley
freshly ground pepper

1 clove garlic, crushed
225 g/1½ cups cooked white fish, eg, cod or haddock, skinned and flaked
50 g/1 cup salt-free soft wholewheat bread crumbs – optional (see page 96)

Preheat the oven to 375°F/190°C.

Mix together the milk, egg yolks, half the cheese, lemon juice and chopped parsley. Season with pepper and crushed garlic. Stir in the fish. Turn the mixture into 4 scallop shells or individual baking dishes and stand on a baking sheet. Sprinkle with the remaining cheese and the bread crumbs, if using, and bake for 10–15 minutes, until golden brown.

Mexican-style eggs

See photograph, page 53

Serves 2

Each serving: 6 mmol (148 mg) sodium; 14 mmol (527 mg) potassium; 162 Kcal

15 ml/1 tbsp polyunsaturated vegetable oil
1 onion, finely chopped
3 tomatoes, sliced

1 green pepper, sliced
2.5 ml/½ tsp chili powder
freshly ground pepper
3 eggs, beaten

Heat the oil in a pan, add the onion, tomatoes and green pepper and cook over moderate heat for 5 minutes. Add the chili powder and season with pepper. Stir in the beaten eggs and cook them over low heat for a few minutes, stirring continuously. Serve immediately.

Spaghetti with pesto sauce

See photograph, page 53

Serves 4

Each serving: negligible sodium; 13 mmol (493 mg) potassium; 470 Kcal

450 g/1 lb wholewheat spaghetti
45 ml/3 tbsp finely chopped fresh
  basil leaves
45 ml/3 tbsp finely chopped fresh
  parsley

2 cloves garlic, crushed
45 ml/3 tbsp olive oil
freshly ground pepper

Cook the spaghetti in plenty of unsalted boiling water for about
12–15 minutes, until just tender.

Meanwhile, prepare the pesto sauce. Combine the basil, parsley
and garlic and pound to a paste. Stir in the olive oil and pepper.
Drain the spaghetti and return it to the pan. Stir in the sauce. Mix
thoroughly and serve immediately.

Pizza

Serves 2–4
Each serving: 2–5 mmol (58–116 mg) sodium; 13–25 mmol
(489–978 mg) potassium; 206–412 Kcal
Using canned tomatoes, each serving: 4–8 mmol (87–114 mg)
sodium; 12–24 mmol (466–932 mg) potassium; 204–408 Kcal

Pizza dough:
120 ml/½ cup warm water
2.5 ml/½ tsp active dry yeast
100 g/1 cup wholewheat flour

Filling:
75 g/¾ cup grated mozzarella cheese
450 g/1 lb tomatoes, sliced

or
1 can (28 oz) tomatoes, drained and
  chopped
1 onion, finely chopped
10 ml/2 tsp dried mixed herbs
15 ml/1 tbsp olive oil
freshly ground pepper

To make the pizza dough, pour the warm water into a small bowl
and sprinkle with the yeast. Stir. Set aside in a warm place for 10–
15 minutes, until frothy. Place the flour in a large bowl, make a
well in the center and pour in the yeast liquid. Mix to a firm dough,
turn on to a lightly floured surface and knead until smooth. Leave
covered in a warm place until doubled in size.

Preheat the oven to 450°F/230°C.

Grease a 28 cm/11 in pizza pan. Roll out the dough and place on
the pizza pan. Sprinkle the cheese on the dough. Add the sliced
tomatoes or canned chopped tomatoes, onion, garlic, herbs and
olive oil. Season with pepper. Bake for 15–20 minutes, then
serve immediately.

Spaghetti with pesto sauce (*top*, see page 51), Mexican-style eggs
(*center*, see page 51), Pizza (*bottom*).

Cracked wheat salad

Serves 4
Each serving: negligible sodium; 10 mmol (377 mg) potassium; 240 Kcal

225 g/1¼ cups cracked wheat
2 small onions, finely chopped
2 tomatoes, finely chopped
30 ml/2 tbsp olive oil
15 ml/1 tbsp lemon juice
30 ml/2 tbsp chopped parsley

freshly ground pepper

Garnish:
lettuce leaves
slices of tomato

Cover the cracked wheat with cold water and soak for 30 minutes. Drain and squeeze out as much water as possible, then spread out on a cloth to dry. Mix the cracked wheat with the onions and tomatoes. Add the olive oil, lemon juice and chopped parsley. Season with pepper. If too dry, add a little water to moisten it.

Line a large serving dish with lettuce leaves and arrange the cracked wheat on top. Decorate with tomato slices. Extra lettuce leaves are served separately to scoop out the salad.

SALADS

Greek cucumber salad

Serves 4
Each serving: 2 mmol (34 mg) sodium; 4 mmol (134 mg) potassium; 27 Kcal

30 ml/2 tbsp low-fat plain yogurt
15 ml/1 tbsp cottage cheese, sieved
15 ml/1 tbsp wine vinegar
15 ml/1 tbsp olive oil
2 cloves garlic, crushed

freshly ground pepper
2 cucumbers, thinly sliced

Garnish:
chopped parsley or chives

Mix together the yogurt, cottage cheese, vinegar, oil and garlic. Season with pepper. Toss the sliced cucumbers in the dressing and garnish with chopped parsley or chives.

Cracked wheat salad (*top*), Greek cucumber salad (*center*), Lentil salad with garlic croûtons (*bottom*, see page 57).

Summer salad

Serves 4
Each serving: negligible sodium; 16 mmol (562 mg) potassium; 171 Kcal

Dressing:
45 ml/3 tbsp olive oil
15 ml/1 tbsp lemon juice
5 ml/1 tsp oregano
freshly ground pepper

Salad:
1 cucumber, sliced
4 tomatoes, quartered

1 green pepper, sliced
1 small onion, finely chopped
50 g/2 oz button mushrooms, sliced
1 small avocado, sliced

Garnish:
chopped chives or
    chopped scallions

Mix together the dressing ingredients. Add the salad vegetables, toss well and garnish with chopped chives or scallions.

Tomato salad

Serves 4
Each serving: negligible sodium; 10 mmol (376 mg) potassium; 44 Kcal

6 large tomatoes, sliced
1 small onion, finely chopped

Dressing:
1 clove garlic, crushed

5 ml/1 tsp chopped basil
5 ml/1 tsp chopped tarragon
30 ml/2 tbsp olive oil
freshly ground pepper

Place the sliced tomatoes in a serving dish. Arrange the chopped onion on top. Stir the crushed garlic and herbs into the olive oil. Season with pepper. Pour the dressing over the tomatoes and serve.

Tossed green salad with curried dressing
See photograph, page 41
Serves 4
Each serving: negligible sodium; 2 mmol (89 mg) potassium; 28 Kcal

pinch dry mustard
pinch light brown sugar
15 ml/1 tbsp wine or cider vinegar
30 ml/2 tbsp polyunsaturated
  vegetable oil

1 clove garlic, crushed
5 ml/1 tsp curry powder
freshly ground pepper
1 lettuce, separated into leaves

Mix together the mustard, sugar and vinegar. Add the oil, garlic and curry powder. Season with pepper. Just before serving, toss the lettuce leaves in the dressing.

Lentil salad with garlic croûtons
See photograph, page 54

Serves 4
Each serving: 1 mmol (30 mg) sodium; 16 mmol (633 mg) potassium; 278 Kcal

225 g/1⅛ cups lentils
1 small onion, chopped
1 small leek, sliced
1 bay leaf

Dressing:
pinch dry mustard
30 ml/2 tbsp wine or cider vinegar
45 ml/3 tbsp polyunsaturated vegetable oil
1 shallot or small onion, finely chopped

freshly ground pepper

Croûtons:
30 ml/2 tbsp polyunsaturated vegetable oil
3 slices salt-free wholewheat bread (see page 94)
2 cloves garlic, crushed

Garnish:
chopped parsley

Put the lentils, onion, leek and bay leaf into a large pan. Add plenty of water, bring to a boil, reduce the heat, cover and simmer for 15–20 minutes, until the lentils are just tender but not mushy. Drain and cool.

To make the dressing, mix together the mustard and vinegar in a serving bowl. Add the oil and the shallot or onion. Season with pepper and stir in the lentils.

To make the croûtons, heat the oil in a skillet, cut the bread into small cubes and fry in the hot oil with the crushed garlic until evenly browned.

Add to the lentil salad, and garnish with chopped parsley.

Rice salad

Serves 6
Each serving: negligible sodium; 8 mmol (298 mg) potassium; 214 Kcal

225 g/1⅛ cups brown short-grain rice
3 tomatoes, chopped
1 green pepper, diced
1 red pepper, diced
1 handful unsalted roasted peanuts (see page 49)

pinch dry mustard
pinch light brown sugar
45 ml/3 tbsp polyunsaturated vegetable oil
2 cloves garlic, finely chopped
5 ml/1 tsp mustard seeds
freshly ground pepper

Dressing:
30 ml/2 tbsp wine or cider vinegar

Cook the rice in 575 ml/2½ cups water for about 30 minutes, until just tender and all the water is absorbed. Cool, then place in a large serving bowl. Stir in the tomatoes, green and red pepper and peanuts.

To make the dressing, mix together the vinegar, mustard and sugar. Add the oil, chopped garlic, mustard seeds and pepper. Mix well. Pour the dressing over the rice and toss.

Waldorf salad

See photograph, page 43

Serves 4
Each serving: 7 mmol (161 mg) sodium; 13 mmol (498 mg) potassium; 213 Kcal

Dressing:
45 ml/3 tbsp olive oil
30 ml/2 tbsp wine or cider vinegar
freshly ground pepper
30 ml/2 tbsp salt-free mayonnaise (see page 48)

Salad:
1 medium-sized head celery, finely chopped
3 crisp red apples, cored and diced
50 g/½ cup walnuts, roughly chopped

Mix together the oil, vinegar and pepper. Stir in the mayonnaise. Add the celery, apples and walnuts and mix well.

VEGETABLE DISHES

Lima beans provençal

Serves 4
Each serving: 1 mmol (25 mg) sodium; 13 mmol (497 mg) potassium; 99 Kcal

900 g/2 lb dry lima beans
15 ml/1 tbsp polyunsaturated vegetable oil
1 onion, sliced
2 cloves garlic, finely chopped

10 ml/2 tsp dried mixed herbs
4 tomatoes, sliced
pinch chili powder
freshly ground pepper

Soak the lima beans overnight in cold water, then boil in plenty of water for 30 minutes. Drain.

Heat the oil in a pan, add the onion, garlic and mixed herbs and cook over moderate heat for about 5 minutes. Stir in the tomatoes and lima beans, season with pepper and a pinch of chili powder. Pour in 100 ml/½ cup water, cover and cook for 25–30 minutes, or until the beans are tender.

Braised red cabbage

Serves 4
Each serving: 4 mmol (84 mg) sodium; 21 mmol (815 mg) potassium; 98 Kcal

15 ml/1 tbsp polyunsaturated vegetable oil
1 medium-sized red cabbage, sliced
1 onion, finely chopped

1 small apple, sliced
225 ml/1 cup water
30 ml/2 tbsp wine vinegar
freshly ground pepper

Heat the oil in a pan, add the cabbage, onion and apple and cook over moderate heat for about 5 minutes. Pour in the water and the vinegar and season with pepper. Bring to a boil, reduce the heat, cover and cook for 35–40 minutes. Stir occasionally and add more water if necessary.

Swiss carrots and potatoes

Serves 4
Each serving: 5 mmol (118 mg) sodium; 24 mmol (931 mg) potassium; 165 Kcal

15 ml/1 tbsp polyunsaturated vegetable oil
1 large onion, finely chopped
450 g/1 lb carrots, pared and cut into strips
450 g/1 lb medium-sized potatoes,

peeled and cut into quarters
50 ml/¼ cup water
freshly ground pepper

Garnish:
chopped parsley

Heat the oil in a pan, add the onion and cook over moderate heat for a few minutes, without browning. Stir in the carrots and potatoes. Pour in the water, season with pepper, cover and simmer for 30–40 minutes, until the water is absorbed.

Turn into a serving dish and sprinkle with chopped parsley.

Spicy chickpea casserole

Serves 4
Each serving: 1 mmol (19 mg) sodium; 20 mmol (767 mg) potassium; 151 Kcal

100 g/½ cup dry chickpeas
15 ml/1 tbsp polyunsaturated vegetable oil
1 large onion, finely chopped
3 cloves garlic, finely chopped
2 cm/1 in piece ginger root, peeled and finely chopped
or
2.5 ml/½ tsp ground ginger
5 ml/1 tsp cumin seeds

5 ml/1 tsp fennel seeds
5 ml/1 tsp mustard seeds
5 ml/1 tsp garam masala
2.5 ml/½ tsp chili powder
1 green pepper, sliced
1 red pepper, sliced (optional)
2 eggplants, sliced
freshly ground pepper
120 ml/½ cup water

Soak the chickpeas overnight in cold water. Drain, then boil in plenty of salt-free water for about 2 hours until tender. Drain again.

Heat the oil in a pan, add the sliced onion, garlic and ginger and cook over moderate heat for 5–10 minutes, without browning. Add the cumin, fennel and mustard seeds and mix well. Stir in the chickpeas, garam masala and chili powder, then the sliced peppers and eggplants. Season with pepper. Pour in the water, cover and cook slowly for 20–25 minutes.

Zucchini casserole

Serves 4
Each serving: 4 mmol (99 mg) sodium; 7 mmol (280 mg) potassium; 146 Kcal

30 ml/2 tbsp polyunsaturated
  vegetable oil
675 g/1½ lb zucchini, thickly sliced
5 ml/1 tsp lemon juice
15 ml/1 tbsp chopped basil

freshly ground pepper
50 g/½ cup grated low-salt cheese
50 g/1 cup salt-free soft wholewheat
  bread crumbs (see page 96)

Preheat the oven to 350°F/180°C.

Heat half the oil in a pan, stir in the zucchini and cook over moderate heat for about 10 minutes. Remove from the heat, add the lemon juice and basil and season with pepper. Place half the zucchini in a baking dish and cover with half the cheese. Add the remaining zucchini and cheese. Fry the bread crumbs in the remaining oil for a few minutes and sprinkle over the zucchini. Bake for about 40 minutes.

Serve hot.

Stuffed zucchini See photograph, page 63

Serves 4
Each serving: 2 mmol (50 mg) sodium; 8 mmol (316 mg) potassium; 144 Kcal

4 medium-sized zucchini
15 ml/1 tbsp polyunsaturated
  vegetable oil
2 tomatoes, diced
225 g/1½ cups fresh corn kernels

15 ml/1 tbsp chopped parsley
freshly ground pepper
25 g/¼ cup grated low-salt cheese
120 ml/½ cup water

Preheat the oven to 375°F/190°C.

Cut the zucchini in half lengthwise and scoop out most of the flesh. Dice the flesh and keep aside for the stuffing. To make the stuffing, heat the oil in a pan, add the zucchini flesh, tomatoes, corn kernels and chopped parsley and cook over moderate heat for 5–10 minutes, stirring occasionally. Season with pepper. Place the zucchini shells in a baking dish, fill with the stuffing, sprinkle with grated cheese, pour the water around the zucchini and bake for 20–25 minutes.

Serve hot.

Lentil curry

Serves 4
Each serving: 1 mmol (25 mg) sodium; 3 mmol (108 mg) potassium; 216 Kcal

15 ml/1 tbsp polyunsaturated
  vegetable oil
2 onions, finely chopped
2 cloves garlic, finely chopped
10 ml/2 tsp ground coriander
5 ml/1 tsp garam masala
5 ml/1 tsp turmeric
5 ml/1 tsp ground cumin
2.5 ml/½ tsp chili powder

225 g/1⅛ cups lentils
300 ml/1¼ cups water
2 bay leaves
3 cloves
freshly ground pepper

Garnish:
fried onion rings

Heat the oil in a pan, add the onions, garlic and the coriander, garam masala, turmeric, cumin and chili, and cook over moderate heat for 10 minutes, stirring occasionally. Stir in the lentils. Pour in the water, add the bay leaves and cloves, season with pepper, cover and simmer for about 20 minutes, or until the lentils are just tender.

To make the garnish, fry the onion rings in a little vegetable oil and arrange on the lentils.

French onion quiche

Serves 2–4
Each serving: 2–4 mmol (44–88 mg) sodium; 12–24 mmol (476–953 mg) potassium; 174–349 Kcal

Quiche dough:
120 ml/½ cup warm water
2.5 ml/½ tsp dry yeast
100 g/1 cup wholewheat flour

Filling:
15 ml/1 tbsp olive oil

450 g/1 lb onions, peeled and sliced
120 ml/½ cup skim milk
1 egg, beaten
freshly ground pepper
grated nutmeg
3 tomatoes, thinly sliced

To make the quiche dough, pour the warm water into a small bowl and sprinkle on the yeast. Stir. Set aside in a warm place for 10–15 minutes, until frothy. Sift the flour into a mixing bowl, make a well in the center, and pour in the yeast liquid. Mix to a firm dough, turn on to a lightly floured surface and knead until smooth. Cover loosely and leave in a warm place until doubled in size.

Preheat the oven to 400°F/200°C.
Grease a 28 cm/11 in pizza pan. Meanwhile, prepare the filling.
Heat the oil in a pan, add the onions, cover and cook over moderate heat for about 20 minutes, stirring occasionally. Transfer the onions to a bowl, add the milk and the egg and mix well. Season with pepper and a little nutmeg. Knead the quiche dough lightly, then roll it out thinly and line the pizza pan. Pour the onion mixture on the dough. Decorate with sliced tomatoes and bake for about 25 minutes, until golden brown.
Serve hot or cold.

Fried rice with vegetables

Serves 4
Each serving: 2 mmol (37 mg) sodium; 14 mmol (548 mg) potassium; 312 Kcal

225 g/1⅛ cups brown short-grain rice
575 ml/2½ cups salt-free, homemade stock (see page 45) or water
30 ml/ 2 tbsp polyunsaturated vegetable oil

2 carrots, finely sliced
1 small green pepper, finely sliced
1 leek, finely sliced
100 g/1½ cups sliced mushrooms
100 g/¾ cup peas, fresh or frozen
freshly ground pepper

Cook the rice in the stock or water for about 30 minutes, until just tender and all the liquid is absorbed. Heat the oil in a pan, stir in the vegetables and cook for a few minutes. Add the rice, mix well and cook over moderate heat for about 10 minutes. Season with pepper.
Serve hot.

Tomatoes provençal

Serves 4
Each serving: negligible sodium; 16 mmol (611 mg) potassium; 45 Kcal

8 large tomatoes
25 g/½ cup soft wholewheat salt-free breadcrumbs (see page 96)

1 shallot or small onion, finely chopped
1 clove garlic, crushed
10 ml/2 tsp dried mixed herbs

Cut a small slice from the top of each tomato. Mix together the bread crumbs, shallot or onion, garlic and mixed herbs. Place one teaspoon of the bread crumb mixture on each tomato and place the tomatoes under a hot broiler for about 5 minutes.

Stuffed zucchini (*top right*, see page 60), Tomatoes provençal (*top left*), Fried rice with vegetables (*bottom*).
OVERLEAF: Broiled stuffed fish (*top*, see page 71), Fish pie (*center*, see page 69), Portuguese fish (*bottom*, see page 70).

Leek quiche

Serves 4
Each serving: 2 mmol (54 mg) sodium; 17 mmol (667 mg) potassium; 344 Kcal

30 ml/2 tbsp polyunsaturated vegetable oil
450 g/1 lb leeks, cut into 1 cm/½ in pieces
1 large onion, sliced
25 g/4 tbsp all-purpose flour

300 ml/1¼ cups skim milk
pinch ground nutmeg
freshly ground pepper
½ recipe wholewheat pastry (see page 92)

Preheat the oven to 350°F/180°C.

Heat the oil in a pan, add the leeks and onion and cook over moderate heat for 15 minutes, without browning. Stir in the flour and gradually add the milk. Stir until the sauce thickens. Season with nutmeg and pepper. Cool slightly.

Grease a 20 cm/8 in pie plate. Roll out the pastry on a lightly floured surface and line the pie plate. Fill with the leek mixture and bake for about 30 minutes until the top is golden brown.

Serve hot or cold.

Stuffed tomatoes

Serves 4
Each serving: 1 mmol (21 mg) sodium; 19 mmol (734 mg) potassium; 100 Kcal

8 large tomatoes
100 g/¾ cup cooked meat (beef, pork, lamb), ground
50 g/1 cup soft wholewheat salt-free bread crumbs (see page 96)

1 small onion, finely chopped
1 clove garlic, crushed
10 ml/2 tsp chopped chives
freshly ground pepper
120 ml/½ cup water

Preheat the oven to 350°F/180°C.

Cut a small slice from each tomato and scoop out the pulp. Mix together the meat, bread crumbs, onion and garlic. Remove the seeds from the tomato pulp, and add the pulp to the meat mixture with the chives. Season with pepper. Fill the tomatoes with the meat mixture, put on the lids and transfer to a baking dish. Pour the water around the tomatoes and bake for 20–25 minutes.

Serve hot.

Leek quiche (*top*), Potato galette (Rosti) (*center*, see page 68), Potato pancakes (*bottom*, see page 68).

Potato galette (Rosti)   See photograph, page 66

Serves 4
Each serving: negligible sodium; 34 mmol (1318 mg) potassium; 303 Kcal

*900 g/2 lb potatoes, scrubbed but
not peeled
1 onion, finely chopped*

*freshly ground pepper
45 ml/3 tbsp polyunsaturated
vegetable oil*

Cook the potatoes in salt-free water for about 20 minutes, or until just tender, but still firm. Cool, then peel and grate the potatoes coarsely. Add the onion and season with pepper.

Heat the oil in a large skillet, add the potato mixture, pressing it down with the back of a spoon. Fry the galette for about 10 minutes over moderate heat until the underside is golden brown. Turn it over by sliding it on to a plate and fry the other side.

When both sides are golden brown, turn on to a hot plate and serve in big chunky wedges.

Potato pancakes   See photograph, page 66

Serves 4
Each serving: negligible sodium; 18 mmol (686 mg) potassium; 172 Kcal

*450 g/1 lb hot cooked potatoes,
mashed
50 g/½ cup wholewheat flour
freshly ground pepper*

*grated nutmeg
15 ml/1 tbsp polyunsaturated
vegetable oil*

Mix together the mashed potatoes and the flour. Season with pepper and some grated nutmeg. Make the potato pancakes immediately to avoid change of color. Heat the oil in a large skillet. Shape the potato mixture into small round flat cakes and cook them for 5–10 minutes on each side.

Serve hot.

New potatoes with garlic and chives

Serves 4
Each serving: 3 mmol (70 mg) sodium; 16 mmol (565 mg) potassium; 188 Kcal

*15 ml/1 tbsp olive oil
675 g/1½ lb small new potatoes,
scrubbed but not peeled*

*2 cloves garlic, crushed
freshly ground pepper
15 ml/1 tbsp chopped chives*

Heat the oil in a large heavy-based pan. Add the potatoes, cover and cook over a moderate heat for about 25 minutes, stirring occasionally. Add the garlic and cook for an additional 5 minutes. Season with pepper, sprinkle with chopped chives and serve hot.

FISH

Fish sticks

Serves 4

Each serving: 5 mmol (106 mg) sodium; 15 mmol (590 mg) potassium; 164 Kcal

450 g/1 lb white fish fillets
45 ml/3 tbsp water
1 bay leaf
225 g/1 cup mashed potatoes (optional)

freshly ground pepper
1 egg, beaten
50 g/½ cup salt-free dry wholewheat bread crumbs (see page 96)

Place the fish in a pan with the water and the bay leaf, cover and cook over moderate heat for about 15 minutes. Drain and cool. Remove the skin and any bones from the fish and flake the flesh. Mix together the fish and potato (if using) and season with pepper. Press the mixture on a lightly floured surface, cut into sticks, dip into the egg and coat with bread crumbs. Broil for about 10 minutes on each side.

Fish pie

See photograph, page 64

Serves 4

Each serving: 6 mmol (130 mg) sodium; 21 mmol (814 mg) potassium; 222 Kcal

450 g/1 lb white fish fillets
300 ml/1¼ cups skim milk
30 ml/2 tbsp polyunsaturated vegetable oil
25 g/4 tbsp all-purpose flour
freshly ground pepper

225 g/1½ cups sliced cooked potatoes
100 g/1½ cups sliced mushrooms
50 g/1 cup salt-free soft wholewheat bread crumbs – optional (see page 96)

Preheat the oven to 375°F/190°C.

Place the fish in a pan, add the milk, bring to a boil, reduce the heat and poach for 5 minutes. Drain and reserve the cooking liquid. Heat the oil in a pan, stir in the flour and gradually add the reserved liquid, stirring continuously until the sauce thickens. Season with pepper.

Mash the potatoes, adding a little skim milk if necessary. Flake the fish and arrange it in a baking dish. Add the mushrooms and pour the sauce over the fish. Pipe the mashed potatoes around the edge of the dish and sprinkle with bread crumbs (if using).

Bake for about 20 minutes, until golden brown, and serve hot.

Portuguese fish

See photograph, page 65

Serves 4
Each serving: 6 mmol (140 mg) sodium; 26 mmol (1010 mg) potassium; 187 Kcal

450 g/1 lb tomatoes, sliced
2 onions, sliced
1 green pepper, sliced
15 ml/1 tbsp olive oil
2 cloves garlic, crushed

15 ml/1 tbsp chopped parsley
675 g/1½ lb piece of white fish
freshly ground pepper
120 ml/½ cup white wine or *water*

Preheat the oven to 350°F/180°C.
Place half the tomatoes, onions, and green pepper in a baking dish. Moisten with the olive oil then add the garlic and parsley. Arrange the fish over the vegetables, season with pepper and cover with the remaining vegetables. Pour in the wine or water, cover with foil and bake for about 40 minutes.

Indian fried fish

Serves 4
Each serving: 6 mmol (130 mg) sodium; 14 mmol (550 mg) potassium; 188 Kcal

2.5 ml/½ tsp turmeric
2.5 ml/½ tsp chili powder
1 clove garlic, crushed
675 g/1½ lb white fish fillets

freshly ground pepper
25 g/4 tbsp all-purpose flour
45 ml/3 tbsp polyunsaturated
*   vegetable oil*

Mix together the turmeric, chili powder and garlic. Divide the fish into 4 portions and press the garlic mixture into the fish. Season with pepper, then coat with flour. Heat the oil in a skillet and fry the fish for 5–10 minutes on each side until golden brown.

Fish German-style

Serves 4
Each serving: 6 mmol (137 mg) sodium; 18 mmol (721 mg) potassium; 172 Kcal

675 g/1½ lb piece of white fish (eg,
*   cod, haddock)*
25 g/⅓ cup rolled oats
15 ml/1 tbsp polyunsaturated
*   vegetable oil*
2.5 ml/½ tsp dry mustard
15 g/1 tbsp chopped parsley

freshly ground pepper
120 ml/½ cup water
10 ml/2 tsp lemon juice
15 ml/1 tbsp wine vinegar
100 g/1½ cups sliced mushrooms
1 small onion, chopped

Preheat the oven to 375°F/190°C.
Cut the fish into 8 pieces and place in a baking dish. Mix

together the rolled oats, oil and mustard. Add the parsley and season with pepper. Spread the mixture over the fish. Mix together the water, lemon juice, vinegar, mushrooms and onion, and pour over the fish.

Cover the dish with foil and bake for about 25 minutes. Remove the foil and bake for an additional 10 minutes.

Broiled stuffed fish   See photograph, page 65

Serves 4
Each serving: 6 mmol (134 mg) sodium; 18 mmol (683 mg) potassium; 150 Kcal

675 g/1½ lb bass, grey mullet or   mackerel
1 onion, finely chopped
1 lemon

2 tomatoes, finely chopped
freshly ground pepper
10 ml/2 tsp chopped thyme
15 ml/1 tbsp olive oil

Stuff the fish with the chopped onion, half the lemon, peeled and finely sliced and the chopped tomatoes. Season with pepper. Sprinkle the thyme over the fish and season with more pepper. Pour the juice of the remaining half lemon and the olive oil over the fish. Marinate for 2 hours. Cook the fish under a hot broiler for about 15–20 minutes, turning once.

Baked fish

Serves 4
Each serving: 6 mmol (137 mg) sodium; 17 mmol (659 mg) potassium; 194 Kcal

12.5 g/1 tbsp unsalted butter
2 onions, finely chopped
15 ml/1 tbsp chopped parsley
675 g/1½ lb piece of cod, halibut or   turbot
50 g/1 cup soft wholewheat salt-free   bread crumbs (see page 96)

120 ml/½ cup water and
120 ml/½ cup white wine
   or
240 ml/1 cup water
freshly ground pepper

Preheat the oven to 350°F/180°C.

Spread the butter on the bottom of a baking dish. Arrange the onions and half the parsley in the dish. Place the fish on top. Sprinkle the bread crumbs over the fish together with the remaining parsley. Pour in the water and white wine, if used, and season with pepper.

Cover with foil and bake for 20 minutes, basting occasionally. Remove the foil and bake for an additional 10 minutes.

MEAT AND POULTRY

Herbed hamburgers See photograph, page 75

Serves 4
Each serving: 4 mmol (99 mg) sodium; 9 mmol (354 mg) potassium; 253 Kcal

450 g/1 lb lean ground beef
1 small onion, finely chopped

10 ml/2 tsp mixed herbs, finely chopped
freshly ground pepper

Mix together the ground beef, onion, mixed herbs and freshly ground pepper. Divide the mixture into 4 large or 8 small equal portions and shape them into round flat cakes. Broil for about 10 minutes on each side.

Serve with a poached egg or a ring of pineapple. For a light meal, serve in a wholewheat roll (see page 95) filled with lettuce, sliced cucumber and tomato.

Spaghetti bolognese

Serves 4
Each serving: 4 mmol (104 mg) sodium; 20 mmol (793 mg) potassium; 638 Kcal

7.5 ml/½ tbsp polyunsaturated vegetable oil
1 small onion, chopped
2 cloves garlic, crushed
10 ml/2 tsp dried mixed herbs
450 g/1 lb lean ground beef
25 g/4 tbsp all-purpose flour
600 ml/2½ cups salt-free stock or water

450 g/1 lb tomatoes, chopped or 400 g/1¾ cups canned tomatoes, chopped
a few fresh basil leaves (optional)
pinch chili powder
freshly ground pepper
450 g/1 lb wholewheat spaghetti

Heat the oil in a pan, add the onion, garlic and mixed herbs and cook over moderate heat for 5–10 minutes, without browning. Add the ground beef and brown lightly all over. Stir in the flour, pour in the stock or water, add the tomatoes and basil leaves, if using, season with chili and pepper and simmer, uncovered, for about 1 hour, stirring occasionally and adding more liquid if necessary. Keep warm or reheat when the spaghetti is ready.

Cook the spaghetti in plenty of unsalted water for 12–15 minutes. Drain, arrange in a warm serving dish and pour the bolognese sauce over it.

Serve with a green salad. Parmesan cheese, sprinkled over the spaghetti, should be avoided or used sparingly as any cheese contains a fair amount of salt.

Moussaká with zucchini

Serves 4
Each serving: 12 mmol (286 mg) sodium; 40 mmol (1566 mg) potassium; 484 Kcal

30 ml/2 tbsp polyunsaturated vegetable oil
2 onions, finely chopped
2 cloves garlic, finely chopped
5 ml/1 tsp dried mixed herbs
450 g/1 lb ground lamb or beef
3 tomatoes, chopped
freshly ground pepper

600 ml/2½ cups salt-free stock or water
450 g/1 lb zucchini, sliced
450 g/1 lb potatoes, peeled and thinly sliced
2 eggs
120 ml/½ cup low-fat plain yogurt
50 g/¼ cup grated Parmesan cheese, (optional)

Preheat the oven to 350°F/180°C.

Heat the oil in a pan, add the onions, garlic and mixed herbs and cook over low heat for a few minutes. Stir in the ground meat and chopped tomatoes and season with pepper. Add stock or water and cook over moderate heat for about 15 minutes.

In a large shallow baking dish arrange alternate layers of zucchini, potatoes and meat mixture, finishing with a layer of potato. Bake for 35–40 minutes.

Meanwhile, beat together the eggs and the yogurt, stir in the cheese if using, pour on to the moussaká and return to the oven for 15–20 minutes, until golden brown.

Beef croquettes

Serves 4
Each serving: 3 mmol (64 mg) sodium; 11 mmol (424 mg) potassium; 214 Kcal

350 g/2½ cups cooked ground beef
1 small onion, finely chopped
1 clove garlic, crushed
10 ml/2 tsp dried mixed herbs

100 g/2 cups soft wholewheat salt-free bread crumbs – optional (see page 96)
5 ml/1 tsp paprika
freshly ground pepper
1 egg, lightly beaten

Mix together the ground cooked beef, onion, garlic, mixed herbs, bread crumbs, if using, paprika and pepper. Add the beaten egg to the beef mixture to bind it. Divide the mixture into 12 and shape into small flat round cakes. Broil for about 10 minutes on each side.

Serve with a spicy tomato sauce (see page 48).

Chili con carne

Serves 4

Each serving: 5 mmol (109 mg) sodium; 28 mmol (1102 mg) potassium; 352 Kcal

225 g/1⅛ cups dry kidney beans
15 ml/1 tbsp polyunsaturated vegetable oil
450 g/1 lb lean chuck steak, cut into 2 cm/1 in cubes
1 onion, finely chopped
3 cloves garlic, finely chopped
5 ml/1 tsp chili powder
1 small green chili pepper, finely chopped (optional)

25 g/4 tbsp all-purpose flour
480 ml/2 cups salt-free stock or water
120 ml/½ cup red wine (optional)
450 g/1 lb fresh tomatoes or 225 g/1 cup canned
5 ml/1 tsp tomato purée
freshly ground pepper

Soak the kidney beans overnight in cold water.

Heat the oil in a pan and fry the beef cubes until evenly brown. Add the onion, garlic, chili powder and chili pepper, if using, and continue cooking for a few minutes, stirring continuously. Stir in the flour. Gradually add the stock or water and wine, if using, the tomatoes and purée, and season with pepper. Bring to a boil, reduce the heat, cover and simmer for about 2½ hours. Stir occasionally during cooking.

Meanwhile, cook the kidney beans in plenty of boiling unsalted water. It is important that the beans are properly boiled for 10 minutes; then cover and simmer for about 1 hour. Drain and add to the stew. Continue cooking until the beans are tender.

Serve with brown rice, couscous or cracked wheat.

Spiced lamb

Serves 4

Each serving: 8 mmol (180 mg) sodium; 19 mmol (676 mg) potassium; 65 Kcal

30 ml/2 tbsp polyunsaturated vegetable oil
675 g/1½ lb boneless lamb, cut into cubes
small piece of cinnamon stick
1 bay leaf
4 cardamom pods
1 onion, finely chopped

6 cloves garlic, finely chopped
2 × 2 cm/1 in cubes ginger root, peeled and finely chopped
25 g/4 tbsp all-purpose flour
2.5 ml/½ tsp cayenne pepper
2.5 ml/½ tsp chili powder
300 ml/1¼ cups plain low-fat yogurt

Preheat the oven to 350°F/180°C.

Heat the oil in a pan and fry the lamb cubes, stirring con-

Chili con carne (*top*), Spiced lamb (*center*), Herbed hamburger (*bottom*, see page 72).

tinuously. Remove the meat and add to the pan the cinnamon, bay leaf and cardamom pods. Stir well. Add the onion, garlic and ginger. Cook over moderate heat for about 10 minutes. Add the meat, stir in the flour, then the cayenne pepper, chili powder and yogurt. Transfer the mixture to an ovenproof dish, cover and bake for about 1½ hours.

Pork kabobs

Serves 4
Each serving: 4 mmol (97 mg) sodium; 21 mmol (816 mg) potassium; 266 Kcal

Marinade:
2.5 ml/½ tsp dry mustard
15 ml/1 tbsp wine vinegar
30 ml/2 tbsp polyunsaturated vegetable oil
5 ml/1 tsp dried mixed herbs
1 clove garlic, finely chopped

freshly ground pepper

Kabobs:
450 g/1 lb pork, diced
1 small green pepper, cut into chunks
4 small onions, peeled and halved
4 tomatoes, halved

Make the marinade by mixing together the mustard, vinegar, oil, mixed herbs, garlic and pepper. Place the meat in a bowl, pour on the marinade, mix well and leave for about 4 hours in a cold place. Thread the diced meat, green pepper, onions and tomatoes alternately on 4 long skewers. Brush with the remaining marinade and cook under a hot broiler for 15–20 minutes, turning occasionally.

Serve with brown rice and tomato sauce (see page 48) or stuffed inside pita bread (see page 96) with lettuce and cucumber.

Crusty roast lamb

Serves 4
Each serving: 5 mmol (111 mg) sodium; 16 mmol (641 mg) potassium; 384 Kcal

1 small leg of lamb
2 cloves garlic, cut into small slivers
50 g/1 cup soft wholewheat salt-free bread crumbs (see page 96)
45 ml/3 tbsp chopped parsley

5 ml/1 tsp dried mixed herbs
15 ml/1 tbsp polyunsaturated vegetable oil
10 ml/2 tsp dry mustard
lemon juice

Trim the lamb, removing as much fat as possible from the top. Make several small incisions all over the lamb and insert a sliver of garlic into each one. Mix together the bread crumbs, parsley and

Crusty roast lamb (*top*), Pork kabobs (*bottom*).

mixed herbs. Mix the oil and mustard and pour on to the bread crumbs. Mix well. Spread the bread crumb mixture all over the top and sides of the joint, pressing it down with your hands. Sprinkle with lemon juice and leave for 2 hours in a cold place.

Preheat the oven to 375°F/190°C.

Roast for about 1½–2 hours.

Rabbit fricassée

Serves 4

Each serving: 6 mmol (135 mg) sodium; 18 mmol (703 mg) potassium; 306 Kcal

30 ml/2 tbsp polyunsaturated vegetable oil
1.3 g/3 lb rabbit, cut into portions
1 large onion, finely chopped
1 carrot, scrubbed and sliced
2 cloves garlic

10 ml/2 tsp dried mixed herbs
freshly ground pepper
15 ml/1 tbsp all-purpose flour
30 ml/2 tbsp wine or sherry
850 ml/3½ cups water

Heat the oil in a pan, add the rabbit pieces and brown all over. Add the onion and carrot and continue cooking over a low heat. Stir in the garlic and mixed herbs and season with pepper. Add the flour and mix well. Gradually stir in the wine or sherry and the water, cover and simmer for about 1½ hours, or until tender.

Chicken tandoori style

Serves 4

Each serving: 8 mmol (195 mg) sodium; 20 mmol (770 mg) potassium; 346 Kcal

8 chicken legs
1 large onion, very finely chopped
4 cloves garlic, very finely chopped
2 cm/1 in piece ginger root, peeled and very finely chopped
10 ml/2 tsp chili powder

10 ml/2 tsp coriander
5 ml/1 tsp ground cumin
60 ml/4 tbsp low-fat plain yogurt
15 ml/1 tbsp lemon juice
15 ml/1 tbsp wine vinegar

Skin the chicken legs and put them in a baking dish. Mix together the onion, garlic and ginger. Add the chili, coriander and cumin and mix well. Spread the spicy mixture over the chicken, pour in the yogurt, lemon juice and vinegar and leave to marinate for about 4 hours.

Preheat the oven to 350°F/180°C.

Cover the dish with foil and bake for about 30 minutes. Remove the foil and bake for an additional 10 minutes.

Roast chicken with herbs

Serves 4
Each serving: 12 mmol (275 mg) sodium; 28 mmol (1103 mg) potassium; 501 Kcal

30 ml/2 tbsp polyunsaturated
  vegetable oil
1 clove garlic, finely chopped
10 ml/2 tsp dried mixed herbs

pinch dry mustard
120 ml/½ cup wine or water
freshly ground pepper
1.3 kg/3 lb chicken

Mix together the oil, garlic, mixed herbs, mustard, wine or water and pepper. Place the chicken in a baking dish, pour the marinade over it and leave for 1–2 hours, turning the chicken occasionally.
  Preheat the oven to 350°F/180°C.
  Roast the chicken for about 1¼ hours, or until cooked through.

Chicken with rice and velouté sauce

Serves 4   See photograph, page 41
Each serving: 14 mmol (314 mg) sodium; 42 mmol (1632 mg) potassium; 708 Kcal

1.3 kg/3 lb chicken
1 large onion, peeled
2 carrots, pared and diced
2 cloves
2 small leeks, cut in half
2 bay leaves
a few peppercorns
1.25 l/5 cups water
30 ml/2 tbsp polyunsaturated
  vegetable oil
225 g/1⅛ cups brown short-grain
  rice

freshly ground pepper

Velouté sauce:
25 g/4 tbps all-purpose flour
1 clove garlic, crushed
10 ml/2 tsp dried mixed herbs
5 ml/1 tsp lemon juice

Garnish:
chopped parsley

Put the chicken into a large pan. Stick the cloves into the peeled onion and add to the chicken together with the diced carrots, leeks, bay leaves and peppercorns. Pour in the water, bring to a boil, reduce the heat, cover and simmer for about 1¼ hours, or until the chicken is tender. Keep the chicken warm. Strain the stock and use for the rice and the velouté sauce.
  Cook the rice: heat half the oil in a pan, add the rice and stir over gentle heat for a few minutes. Add about half the reserved strained chicken stock, and season with pepper. Bring to a boil, reduce the heat, cover and simmer for about 30 minutes, or until the stock has been absorbed and the rice is just tender.
  To make the velouté sauce, heat the remaining oil in a pan, stir in the flour and gradually add the remaining strained stock, stirring continuously. Bring to a boil, reduce the heat, add the garlic,

mixed herbs and lemon juice. Season with pepper and continue cooking over gentle heat for 5–10 minutes.

Place the rice in a warm serving dish, carve the chicken and arrange it over the rice. Pour the sauce over the chicken and decorate with chopped parsley.

Chicken pie

Serves 4

Each serving: 2 mmol (51 mg) sodium; 12 mmol (452 mg) potassium; 584 Kcal

1 recipe flaky pastry (see page 93)
15 ml/1 tbsp polyunsaturated
* vegetable oil*
25 g/4 tbsp all-purpose flour
550 ml/2¼ cups salt-free chicken
* stock (see page 45)*
225 g/1⅓ cups cooked diced chicken

100 g/1½ cups sliced mushrooms
1 small red pepper, finely chopped
1 clove garlic, finely chopped
120 ml/½ cup white wine
* (optional)*
freshly ground pepper
pinch chili powder

Preheat the oven to 375°F/190°C.

Grease a 20 cm/8 in pie plate. Roll out half the pastry on a lightly floured surface and line the pie plate. Reserve the other half of the pastry to cover the top.

Prepare the filling. Heat the oil in a pan, stir in the flour and gradually add the stock, stirring continuously, until the sauce thickens. Stir in the chicken, mushrooms, red pepper and garlic. Add the wine (if using). Season with pepper and a pinch of chili powder. Cook for 5–10 minutes over moderate heat.

Spoon the chicken mixture into the pie shell. Roll out the remaining pastry and cover the top, brushing the edges with water to seal them.

Bake for about 30 minutes, or until the pastry is lightly browned.

DESSERTS

Fresh pineapple water ice

Serves 4   See photograph, page 87
Each serving: negligible sodium; 6 mmol (251 mg) potassium;
144 Kcal

100 g/½ cup sugar   *10 ml/2 tsp unflavored gelatin*
1 fresh ripe pineapple, halved   *480 ml/2 cups water*
  lengthwise

Heat the water and the sugar in a pan until the sugar has dissolved.
Bring to a boil and boil rapidly for a few minutes or until the
volume is reduced by half. Cool.

Scoop out the flesh of the pineapple. Reserve the shells and chill
in the refrigerator until serving time. Purée the flesh in an electric
blender, or chop finely. Place 150 ml/⅝ cup of the cooled syrup in
a bowl, stir in the gelatin and leave for a few minutes. Stand the
bowl in a pan of hot water and heat gently until the gelatin has dissolved. Stir in the remaining syrup and leave until cold. Mix
together the syrup and pineapple purée, pour into a freezer container, cover and freeze for 1–2 hours, until slushy.

Remove the mixture from the freezer, beat thoroughly and
return to the freezer for at least 2 hours, or until firm.

Stand the water ice at room temperature for about 15 minutes
to soften slightly, then scoop into the chilled pineapple shells.
Serve immediately.

Pear pie   See photograph, page 87

Serves 4
Each serving: negligible sodium; 7 mmol (282 mg) potassium;
503 Kcal

1 recipe white shortcrust pastry (see   *50 g/½ cup coarsely chopped walnuts*
  page 92)   *50 g/¼ cup brown sugar*
450 g/1 lb ripe pears, pared and   *5 ml/1 tsp cinnamon*
  sliced   *a few drops vanilla extract*

Preheat the oven to 350°F/180°C.

Divide the pastry in half, then on a lightly floured surface roll
out one half and line a 23 cm/9 in pie plate. Place the fruit over the
pastry. Add the chopped walnuts and sprinkle with sugar, cinnamon and vanilla extract. Moisten the edges of the pastry. Roll
out the remaining half, cover the pie and trim and pinch the edges

to seal them. Trimmings of pastry can be cut into leaf shapes and placed on top to decorate the pie. Bake for 30–35 minutes.
    Serve hot or cold.

Variation   The potassium content is higher if wholewheat flour is used.

French plum tart   See photograph, page 41

Serves 6–8
Each serving: 1–2 mmol (25–33 mg) sodium; 8–10 mmol (296–394 mg) potassium; 283–378 Kcal

1 recipe white shortcrust pastry (see page 92)

Filling:
900 g/2 lb ripe plums, pitted and cut in half
1 egg

50 g/¼ cup granulated sugar
25 g/4 tbsp all-purpose flour
a few drops vanilla extract
240 ml/1 cup skim milk

Topping:
25 g/2 tbsp brown sugar

Preheat the oven to 350°F/180°C.
    Roll out the pastry on a lightly floured surface and line a 28 cm/ 11 in tart pan. Arrange the fruit over the pastry.
    Mix together the egg and the sugar. Stir in the flour and vanilla extract and pour in the milk gradually, stirring continuously. Pour the custard over the fruit and bake for 35–40 minutes. Cool slightly and sprinkle with brown sugar.
    Serve hot or cold.

Variations   The custard filling can be omitted.
The potassium content is higher if wholewheat flour is used.

Summer fruit salad   See photograph, page 86

Serves 4
Each serving: negligible sodium; 13 mmol (503 mg) potassium; 118 Kcal

juice of 1 large orange
50 g/¼ cup sugar
120 ml/½ cup water
1 small melon, skinned, seeded and diced

225 g/1¼ cups strawberries, hulled and sliced
3 peaches, skinned, pitted and sliced

Place the orange juice, sugar and water in a pan and heat slowly until the sugar has dissolved. Bring to a boil and boil rapidly for a few minutes, until syrupy. Cool.
    Place the fruit in a serving bowl, pour the syrup in and mix gently.
    Serve as soon as possible.

Winter fruit salad

Serves 4

Each serving: negligible sodium; 26 mmol (605 mg) potassium; 246 Kcal

120 ml/½ cup water
50 g/¼ cup sugar
2 oranges, peeled, sliced and seeded
225 g/½ lb seedless green grapes,
* halved*

2 bananas, peeled and sliced
2 eating apples
juice of ½ lemon
50 g/½ cup shelled walnuts
15 ml/1 tbsp kirsch (optional)

Place the water and the sugar in a pan and heat over moderate heat until the sugar has dissolved. Bring to a boil and boil rapidly for a few minutes, until syrupy. Cool.

Place the oranges, grapes and bananas in a serving bowl. Peel, core and slice the apples and sprinkle with lemon juice to prevent discoloration. Add to the other fruit together with the walnuts. Pour the cool syrup in, add the kirsch, if using, and mix gently.

Serve as soon as possible.

Savarin   See photograph, page 86

Serves 4–6

Each serving: 2–3 mmol (52–77 mg) sodium; 6–8 mmol (220–331 mg) potassium; 399–599 Kcal

Batter:
30 ml/2 tbsp sugar
300 ml/1¼ cups warm skim milk
12.5 g/2 packages dry yeast
250 g/1¼ cups bread flour
100 g/½ cup polyunsaturated salt-free
* margarine, melted*

2 eggs, beaten

Filling:
100 g/½ cup sugar
120 ml/½ cup water
fresh fruit, eg, strawberries,
* raspberries, pineapple, peaches*

To make the batter, dissolve 5 ml/1 teaspoon of the sugar in the warm milk. Sprinkle on the yeast, stir and leave in a warm place for 10–15 minutes, until the liquid becomes frothy. Place the flour and remaining sugar in a large bowl. Make a well in the center, pour in the melted margarine and the yeast liquid, add the beaten eggs, and beat with a wooden spoon for about 5 minutes.

Preheat the oven to 400°F/200°C.

Turn the batter into a greased and floured 23 cm/9 in savarin mold and leave in a warm place for 10 minutes.

Bake for about 35 minutes, until golden brown and well-risen. Cool.

To make the filling, dissolve the sugar in the water over low heat. Bring to a boil and boil for a few minutes. Pour over the savarin.

Prepare the fruit and pile in the center. Serve soon after adding the fruit.

Orange and date fruit salad

Serves 4
Each serving: negligible sodium; 8 mmol (297 mg) potassium;
257 Kcal

50 g/¼ cup sugar
120 ml/½ cup water
1.25 ml/¼ tsp vanilla extract
2 oranges, peeled, sliced into rings and seeded

75 g/½ cup whole dates, pitted and chopped
2 eating apples
juice of ½ lemon
50 g/½ cups slivered almonds

Place the sugar, water and vanilla extract in a pan and heat slowly until the sugar has dissolved. Bring to a boil and boil rapidly for a few minutes, until syrupy. Cool.

Place the oranges and dates in a serving bowl. Core the apples, then slice them and sprinkle with lemon juice to prevent discoloration. Add to the fruit in the bowl. Pour the sugar syrup over the fruit.

Place the almonds under a hot broiler for a few minutes, then sprinkle over the orange salad.

Serve as soon as possible.

Orange chocolate cake (*top*, see page 89), Orange and date fruit salad (*center and bottom*).
OVERLEAF: Savarin (*top left*, see page 83), Pear pie (*top right*, see page 81), Summer fruit salad (*bottom left and center*, see page 82), Fresh pineapple water ice (*bottom right*, see page 81).

PASTRY AND BAKING

Orange chocolate cake   See photograph, page 85

Makes 8 slices
Each slice: 1 mmol (19 mg) sodium; 3 mmol (109 mg) potassium;
350 Kcal

100 g/½ cup polyunsaturated salt-
free margarine
100 g/½ cup sugar
2 eggs, beaten
50 g/2 squares semi-sweet chocolate,
grated
30 ml/2 tbsp fresh orange juice
50 g/½ cup chopped walnuts
(optional)

125 g/1¼ cups all-purpose flour
5 ml/1 tsp baking powder substitute
(see page 97)

Frosting:
175 g/¾ cup confectioner's sugar
30 ml/2 tbsp fresh orange juice
peel of 1 orange, cut into strips and
blanched

Preheat the oven to 350°F/180°C.
Beat together the margarine and sugar until light and fluffy.
Add the eggs gradually, beating well after each addition. Stir in the
grated chocolate and fresh orange juice. Add the walnuts, if using.
Sift the flour with the baking powder substitute and stir into the
egg mixture.
Pour into a greased 18 cm/7 in round cake pan and bake for 30–40
minutes, or until a wooden toothpick pierced through the center
comes out clean. Cool before turning out. Make up the frosting
with the orange juice, pour over the cake and decorate with
the peel.

Shortbread

Makes about 16 cookies
Each cookie: negligible sodium; negligible potassium; 93 Kcal

100 g/1 cup all-purpose flour
50 g/⅜ cup rice flour
50 g/¼ cup sugar
100 g/½ cup unsalted butter

Decoration:
5 ml/1 tsp superfine sugar

Almond cake (*top*, see page 90), Two-cereal bread (*center*, see page
94), Sesame bars (*bottom*, see page 91).

Preheat the oven to 325°F/170°C.

Sift the flours into a bowl and add the sugar. Cut the butter into small pieces and gradually work it into the dry ingredients until it becomes a smooth dough. Transfer to a 18 cm/7 in square or round pan. Bake for about 30 minutes, until lightly golden.

Sprinkle the superfine sugar on top and cool in the pan for a few minutes. Cut into small bars and cool completely before removing from the pan.

Variation   The potassium content could be increased if wholewheat flour were used instead of white flour.

Almond cake   See photograph, page 88

Makes 12 slices
Each slice: 1 mmol (18 mg) sodium; 3 mmol (108 mg) potassium; 249 Kcal

175 g/¾ cup polyunsaturated salt-free margarine
175 g/¾ cup sugar
3 eggs, beaten
175 g/1½ cups all-purpose flour
5 ml/1 tsp baking powder substitute (see page 97)

100 g/1 cup ground almonds
1.25 ml/¼ tsp almond extract

Decoration:
confectioner's sugar

Preheat the oven to 350°/180°C.

Beat together the margarine and the sugar until light and fluffy. Add the eggs, a little at a time, and beat well after each addition. Sift together the flour and baking powder substitute, add the ground almonds and almond extract and gradually stir into the egg mixture.

Pour the mixture into a greased 20 cm/8 in cake pan and bake for about 40 minutes, or until a wooden toothpick pierced through the center comes out clean.

Cool in the pan before turning it out, then sprinkle confectioner's sugar over the top.

Variation   The potassium content can be increased by using wholewheat flour instead of white.

Wholewheat cookies

Makes about 24
Each cookie: negligible sodium; 1 mmol (40 mg) potassium; 61 Kcal

175 g/1½ cups wholewheat flour
50 g/⅔ cup rolled oats
5 ml/1 tsp baking powder substitute (see page 97)
25 g/2 tbsp light brown sugar

75 g/6 tbsp polyunsaturated salt-free margarine
60 ml/4 tbsp skim milk, approximately

Preheat the oven to 375°F/190°C.

Mix together the flour, rolled oats and baking powder substitute. Rub in the margarine until the mixture looks like bread crumbs, then stir in the sugar. Add the milk and mix to a firm dough. Turn on to a lightly floured surface and roll out thinly, then cut into 6 cm/2½ in circles. Prick with a fork a few times. Transfer to a greased baking sheet and bake for about ·15–20 minutes.

Cool on a wire rack.

Sesame bars

See photograph, page 88

Makes about 24

Each cookie: negligible sodium; 1 mmol (45 mg) potassium; 88 Kcal

175 g/2¼ cups rolled oats
50 g/⅓ cup sesame seeds, roasted
90 ml/6 tbsp polyunsaturated
  vegetable oil

45 ml/3 tbsp clear honey
50 g/¼ cup light brown sugar

Preheat the oven to 350°F/180°C.

Mix all the ingredients together. Press into a well greased jelly roll pan and smooth the top. Bake for about 20 minutes. Cool in the pan for a few minutes, then cut into bars and cool completely before removing from the pan.

Apple cake

Makes 8 slices

Each slice: 1 mmol (20 mg) sodium; 4 mmol (138 mg) potassium; 167 Kcal

2 eggs
75 g/⅓ cup sugar
75 g/¾ cup all-purpose flour
2.5 ml/½ tsp baking powder substitute
  (see page 97)

Filling:
675 g/1½ lb cooking apples, pared,
  cored and sliced
50 g/¼ cup light brown sugar
25 g/2 tbsp polyunsaturated salt-free
  margarine
10 ml/2 tsp cinnamon

Preheat the oven to 350°F/180°C.

Beat together the eggs and the sugar until light and creamy. Sift the flour and baking powder substitute and fold into the egg mixture. Pour the mixture into a greased 18 cm/7 in round cake pan.

Divide the apples, sugar, margarine and cinnamon into 3 parts and arrange a third of the apples on the dough. Sprinkle with a third of the sugar, cinnamon and margarine, cut into small pieces. Repeat twice. Bake for 40–45 minutes.

Variation   Potassium content will be increased by 7 mmol per slice if wholewheat flour is used.

Shortcrust pastry (using margarine only)

Per ¼ recipe: negligible sodium; 2 mmol (80 mg) potassium; 380 Kcal

225 g/2 cups all-purpose flour
100 g/½ cup salt-free polyunsaturated margarine

approximately 90 ml/6 tbsp cold water

Place the flour in a bowl. Cut the margarine into small pieces and add to the flour. Rub the margarine into the flour until it looks like fresh bread crumbs. Add water gradually and mix to a soft, smooth dough. If it is sticky, add a little flour. The pastry can be used immediately.

Shortcrust pastry (using oil and margarine)

Per ¼ recipe: negligible sodium; 2 mmol (79 mg) potassium; 356 Kcal

225 g/2 cups all-purpose flour
50 g/4 tbsp polyunsaturated salt-free margarine

30 ml/2 tbsp polyunsaturated vegetable oil
approximately 90 ml/6 tbsp cold water

Place the flour in a bowl. Cut the margarine into small pieces and add to flour. Rub the margarine into the flour until it looks like fresh bread crumbs. Add the oil and mix well. Pour in water gradually and mix to a soft, smooth dough. The pastry can be used immediately.

Wholewheat pastry (using margarine only)

Per ¼ recipe: negligible sodium; 5 mmol (204 mg) potassium; 362 Kcal

225 g/2 cups wholewheat flour
100 g/½ cup salt-free polyunsaturated margarine

approximately 90 ml/6 tbsp cold water

Place the flour in a bowl. Cut the margarine into small pieces and add to the flour. Rub the margarine into the flour until it looks like fresh bread crumbs. Add water gradually and mix to a soft, smooth dough. The pastry is best chilled for 30 minutes before using.

Wholewheat pastry (using oil and margarine)

Per ¼ recipe: negligible sodium; 5 mmol (204 mg) potassium; 371 Kcal

225 g/2 cups wholewheat flour
50 g/4 tbsp polyunsaturated salt-free margarine

45 ml/3 tbsp polyunsaturated vegetable oil
approximately 90 ml/6 tbsp cold water

Place the flour in a bowl. Cut the margarine into small pieces and add to flour. Rub the margarine into the flour until it looks like fresh bread crumbs. Add the oil and mix well. Pour in water a little at a time, and mix to a soft, smooth dough. The pastry is best chilled for 30 minutes before using.

Flaky pastry

Per ¼ recipe: negligible sodium; 2 mmol (80 mg) potassium; 425 Kcal

125 g/⅝ cup polyunsaturated salt-free margarine
225 g/2 cups all-purpose flour

approximately 120 ml/8 tbsp cold water

Divide the margarine into 4 equal portions. Place the flour in a bowl and rub one quarter of the margarine into it until it resembles fresh bread crumbs. Mix to a soft dough with the water.

On a lightly floured surface, roll the pastry into a rectangle. Place another quarter of the margarine over it, cut into small pieces. Fold the bottom third up and the top third of the pastry down, seal the edges and turn it so that the folds are now at the sides. Roll again, put another quarter of margarine over it and repeat in the same way until all the margarine has been used up. Chill the pastry in the refrigerator at least 30 minutes before using.

BREADMAKING

As any bread bought in a bakery contains salt it is important that you should try to bake your own bread. With a little practice, breadmaking becomes easy provided you follow a few simple rules.

- When baking wholewheat bread, make sure that you use 100 per cent stoneground wholewheat flour to ensure that it is salt-free.
- Dissolve the dry yeast in warm water or milk (110°F/43°C) and leave in a warm place for about 10 minutes, until frothy.

A little sugar in the water helps the yeast to activate.

Dry yeast has been used for all the bread recipes in this book as fresh yeast is more difficult to find and keeps for only a few days. If, however, you wish to use fresh yeast you will need twice the quantity of dry yeast.

- When the yeast is frothy, add to the flour and other ingredients and mix to a dough. Transfer the dough to a lightly floured surface and knead for 5–10 minutes.
- Place the dough in a lightly floured bowl, cover loosely and leave in a warm place until it has doubled in size. Depending on the kind of dough and the ingredients used, it will take between 30 minutes and 1½ hours.
- Knead the dough once again, then shape and transfer to a greased baking pan or sheet and cover loosely.
- Leave to rise again. This will usually take between 15 and 30 minutes.
- Bake in a hot oven.

Wholewheat bread

Makes 1 loaf, 12 slices
Each slice: negligible sodium; 6 mmol (145 mg) potassium; 133 Kcal

5 ml/1 tsp sugar
240 ml/1 cup lukewarm water
10 ml/2 tsp dry yeast
450 g/4 cups wholewheat flour

30 ml/2 tbsp bran
12.5 g/1 tbsp salt-free poly-
*   unsaturated margarine*

Dissolve the sugar in 120 ml/½ cup of the lukewarm water. Sprinkle on the yeast, stir well and leave in a warm place for 10 minutes, until frothy. Place the flour and bran in a large bowl and rub in the margarine. Pour in the frothy yeast liquid and the remainder of the water. Mix to a dough, adding more flour if necessary. Transfer to a lightly floured surface and knead for 5–10 minutes, until smooth and elastic. Cover loosely and leave in a warm place until it has doubled in size.

Turn out the dough and knead again for a few minutes. Grease a 450 g/1 lb loaf pan and shape the dough to fit the pan. Leave covered in a warm place for about 30 minutes.

Preheat the oven to 425°F/220°C and bake the bread for 30–40 minutes, until it is golden brown and sounds hollow when tapped underneath.

Cool on a wire rack.

Two-cereal bread   See photograph, page 88

Makes 2 loaves, 12 slices each
Each slice: negligible sodium; 4 mmol (149 mg) potassium; 133 Kcal

5 ml/1 tsp sugar
600 ml/2½ cups (approx) lukewarm water
20 ml/4 tsp dry yeast
675 g/5¾ cups wholewheat flour
225 g/2 cups rye flour

60 ml/4 tbsp bran
25 g/2 tbsp salt-free polyunsaturated margarine

Decoration:
cracked wheat

Dissolve the sugar in 120 ml/½ cup lukewarm water. Sprinkle on the yeast, stir well and leave in a warm place for 10 minutes, until frothy.

Place the flours and bran in a large bowl and rub in the margarine. Pour in the frothy yeast liquid and approximately 480 ml/2 cups lukewarm water. Mix to a dough, adding more flour if necessary. Transfer to a lightly floured surface and knead for 5–10 minutes until smooth and elastic. Cover lightly and leave in a warm place until it has doubled in size.

Turn out the dough and knead again for a few minutes. Grease a baking sheet. Divide the dough into two and shape each one into a ball. Place on the baking sheet. Score the loaves with a sharp knife in a lattice pattern, brush with water and sprinkle with cracked wheat. Leave covered in a warm place for about 30 minutes.

Preheat the oven to 425°F/220°C and bake the bread for 40–50 minutes.

Cool on a wire rack.

Breakfast rolls

Makes 12
Each roll: negligible sodium; 4 mmol (160 mg) potassium; 204 Kcal

5 ml/1 tsp sugar
450 ml/1⅞ cups lukewarm water
15 ml/3 tsp dry yeast
450 g/4 cups wholewheat flour
225 g/2 cups bread flour

25 g/2 tbsp salt-free polyunsaturated margarine

Decoration:
sesame seeds

Dissolve the sugar in 120 ml/½ cup lukewarm water. Sprinkle on the yeast, stir well and leave in a warm place for 10 minutes, until frothy.

Place the flours in a large bowl and rub in the margarine. Pour in the frothy yeast liquid and approximately 330 ml/1⅜ cups water and mix to a dough, adding more flour if necessary. Transfer to a lightly floured surface and knead for 5–10 minutes until smooth and elastic. Cover lightly and leave in a warm place until it has doubled in size.

Turn out the dough and knead again for a few minutes. Grease a large baking sheet. Divide the dough into 12 pieces and shape each one into a round roll. Brush with water and sprinkle with sesame seeds. Leave covered in a warm place for about 30 minutes.

Preheat the oven to 425°F/220°C and bake the bread for about 20 minutes until golden brown.
Cool on a wire rack.

Pita bread

Makes 8
Each pita: negligible sodium; 4 mmol (138 mg) potassium; 189 Kcal

5 ml/1 tsp sugar
approximately 240 ml/1 cup luke-
    warm water
10 ml/2 tsp dry yeast
225 g/2 cups wholewheat flour
225 g/2 cups bread flour

Dissolve the sugar in 120 ml/½ cup lukewarm water. Sprinkle on the yeast, stir well and leave in a warm place for 10 minutes, until frothy.

Place the flours in a large bowl and pour in the frothy yeast liquid and approximately 120 ml/½ cup lukewarm water. Mix to a dough, adding more flour if necessary. Transfer to a lightly floured surface and knead for 5–10 minutes, until smooth and elastic. Cover lightly and leave in a warm place until it has doubled in size.

Turn out the dough and knead again for a few minutes. Grease 2 baking sheets. Divide the dough into 8 pieces and shape each one into a smooth, seamless ball. Space the pita balls on a floured surface and allow to rest, covered, for 10 minutes.

Preheat the oven to 425°F/220°C. Flatten 2 or 3 balls into ovals 20 cm/8 in long, lift them on to a greased baking sheet and bake for 5–10 minutes until lightly browned.

Repeat the process until all the pitas are baked.

Note: Do not flatten the other balls until there is room in the oven for them to be baked as they will rise prematurely and be difficult to handle.

Serving suggestions Pitas are usually halved, split open and filled with salad and meat.

Bread crumbs

per 25 g/½ cup wholewheat fresh: negligible sodium; 1 mmol (55 mg) potassium; 54 Kcal
per 25 g/½ cup white fresh: negligible sodium; 1 mmol (55 mg) potassium; 58 Kcal

Leftover salt-free wholewheat or white
    bread

Preheat the oven to 325°F/170°C.
Place the bread in an electric blender or coffee grinder and

switch it on for a few minutes. The bread can also be crumbled by hand. Place the crumbs on a baking sheet and bake for 15–20 minutes, stirring occasionally. Cool and store in an airtight container.

Variations For fine bread crumbs, rub the baked crumbs through a sieve.
For fresh bread crumbs, omit the baking process.

Baking powder substitute

To be made by a pharmacy:

potassium bicarbonate 39.8 g
starch 28.0 g

tartaric acid 7.5 g
potassium bitartrate 56.1 g

Use 1 heaped tsp per 225 g/2 cups all-purpose flour.

Alternatively you may find a commercially produced salt-free baking powder, in some health shops.

Wholewheat scones

Makes about 12
Each scone: negligible sodium; 2 mmol (68 mg) potassium; 32 Kcal

225 g/4 tbsp plain wholewheat flour
5 ml/1 tsp baking powder substitute
  (see above)
approximately 90 ml/6 tbsp cold
  water

50 g/4 tbsp polyunsaturated salt-free
  margarine
skim milk for glazing

Preheat the oven to 425°F/220°C.
   Sift the flour and baking powder substitute into a bowl. Rub in the margarine until the mixture looks like bread crumbs. Add water gradually and mix to a soft dough. Turn on to a lightly floured surface and roll out to a 2 cm/¾ in thickness. Cut into 5 cm/2 in circles and brush with a little skim milk. Transfer to a floured baking sheet and bake for 10–15 minutes.
   Cool on a wire rack.

Date and apple scones

Makes about 12
Each scone: negligible sodium; 1 mmol (46 mg) potassium;
109 Kcal

225 g/2 cups all-purpose flour
5 ml/1 tsp baking powder substitute
(see page 97)
2.5 ml/½ tsp allspice
50 g/4 tbsp polyunsaturated salt-free
margarine

25 g/2 tbsp light brown sugar
50 g/⅓ cup chopped dates
1 small cooking apple pared, cored
and grated
45 ml/3 tbsp skim milk,
approximately

Preheat the oven to 425°F/220°C.

Sift the flour, baking powder substitute and allspice into a bowl.
Rub in the margarine until it looks like bread crumbs. Add the
sugar, dates and apple and mix well. Add the milk gradually and
mix to a soft dough. Turn on to a lightly floured surface and roll
out to a 2 cm/¾ in thickness. Cut into 5 cm/2 in circles. Transfer to
a floured baking sheet and bake for 10–15 minutes.

Cool on a wire rack.

The sodium and potassium content of common foods

Vegetables

Note: All vegetables cooked are without salt

	Wt (g)	Handy measure	Sodium mg	Sodium mmol	Potassium mmol	Kcal
Asparagus	100	6 spears	2	tr	7.1	26
Beans, baked, canned in tomato sauce	125	½ cup	579	25.2	6.7	152
Beans, lima, boiled	115	½ cup	271	11.8	6.5	110
Beans, green, boiled	65	½ cup	tr	tr	2.4	19
Beans, kidney, raw	100	½ cup	10	0.4	25.2	343
Beets, cooked	83	½ cup, diced	36	1.6	4.4	27
Broccoli, cooked	100	1 large stalk	10	0.4	6.9	26
Brussels sprouts, cooked	100	6 to 7 sprouts	10	0.4	7.0	36
Cabbage, red, raw	100	1 cup, shredded	26	1.1	6.9	31
Cabbage, cooked	100	³/₅ cup	14	0.6	4.2	20
Carrots, cooked	100	⅔ cup	33	1.4	5.7	31
Cauliflower, cooked	100	1 cup	9	0.4	5.3	22
Celery, raw	20	1 (5 in stalk)	25	1.1	1.7	3
Chickpeas (garbanzos)	100	½ cup, dry	26	1.1	20.4	360
Corn on the cob	200	4 in cob	tr	tr	5.0	100
Corn, canned kernels	100	²/₅ cup	236	10.3	2.5	66
Leeks, cooked	100	3 to 4 (5 in long)	5	0.2	8.9	52
Lentils, raw	100	½ cup, dry	41	1.8	20.6	345
Lettuce, raw	100	3½ oz	9	0.4	6.8	14
Mushrooms, raw	100	4 large	15	0.6	10.6	28
Onions, raw	100	1 small (2 ¼ diameter)	10	0.4	4.0	38
Parsnips, cooked	100	½ cup, diced	8	0.3	9.7	66
Peas, canned	100	¾ cup	236	10.3	2.5	88
Peppers, green, raw	100	1 large shell	13	0.6	5.5	22
Potatoes, boiled	100	1 small	2	tr	7.3	65
Potatoes, baked with skin	100	1 small	3	tr	10.4	76
Potatoes, french fries	50	10 pieces	4	tr	16.7	110
Potatoes, instant, made-up	210	1 cup	491	21.4	18.1	166
Potatoes, chips, salted	20	10 pieces	380	16.5	6.8	113
Radishes	100	10 small	18	0.8	8.3	17
Rutabaga, cooked	100	½ cup, cubed	4	tr	4.3	35
Sauerkraut	100	⅔ cup	747	32.5	3.6	18
Spinach, cooked	90	½ cup	45	2.0	7.5	21
Squash, acorn	195	½ squash, baked	2	tr	19.2	86
Squash, butternut	205	1 cup, baked	2	tr	32.0	139
Squash, hubbard	205	1 cup, baked	2	tr	14.3	103

	Wt (g)	Handy measure	Sodium mg	Sodium mmol	Potassium mmol	Kcal
Sweet potato, baked in skin	180	1 large	15	0.6	9.4	172
Tomato, raw	100	1 (2 in diameter)	3	tr	6.3	22
Yam, cooked	100	½ cup	16	0.7	7.7	105

Fruit

Apple	150	1 medium (2½ in diameter)	1	tr	4.2	87
Applesauce	100	⅓ cup	2	tr	2.0	41
Apricots, raw	100	2 to 3 medium	1	tr	7.2	51
Apricots, dried	50	8 halves	13	0.6	12.3	130
Avocado	100	½ medium (3¼ × 4 in)	4	tr	15.5	167
Banana	100	6 in long	1	tr	9.5	85
Blackberries	144	1 cup, raw	1	tr	6.3	84
Cherries	100	15 large	2	tr	4.9	70
Dates, dried	178	1 cup, pitted	2	tr	29.5	488
Figs, dried	30	2 small	10	0.4	4.9	82
Fruit cocktail, canned	100	½ cup	5	0.2	4.3	37
Grapes	50	11 medium	2	tr	2.1	35
Grapefruit, fresh	100	½ medium, pink	1	tr	3.5	40
Mangoes, raw	100	½ medium	7	0.3	4.8	66
Melon balls, honeydew	230	1 cup	21	0.9	11.1	143
Nectarines, raw	50	1 medium	3	tr	7.5	32
Olives, green	7	1	156	6.8	tr	7
Orange	150	1 medium (3 in diameter)	2	tr	7.7	73
Peach	100	1 medium	1	tr	5.2	38
Pear	200	1 medium	4	tr	6.7	112
Pineapple, fresh	84	1 slice (3½ in diameter)	1	tr	3.1	44
Plums, raw	100	2 medium	2	tr	7.7	66
Prunes, dried	100	8 large	tr	tr	0.3	344
Raisins	10	1 tbsp	3	tr	1.9	29
Raspberries	100	¾ cup	1	tr	4.3	57
Rhubarb, raw	100	¾ cup, cubed	2	tr	6.4	16
Strawberries	100	10 large	1	tr	4.2	37
Tangerines	170	1 large	2	tr	3.2	46

Meat, poultry and fish

Bacon, boiled lean	21	1 strip	442	19.2	2.3	65
Beef, ground, raw weight	86	2 tbsp, to make 1 patty	41	1.8	12.3	140
Beef, rump steak, broiled lean	37	2 slices, thin	18	0.8	3.9	77
Beef, roast, lean	80	1 slice	34	1.5	9.5	173
Bologna	28	1 slice	364	15.8	1.6	88
Chicken drumstick	80	2 small	79	3.4	8.3	126
Chicken, roast, lean	100	3½ oz	50	2.2	8.2	117
Corned beef, medium fat	28	1 slice	268	11.6	0.4	60
Frankfurter	50	1 large	550	23.9	2.8	128
Lamb, chop, lean	61	2 thin slices	43	1.9	6.5	144

	Wt (g)	Handy measure	Sodium mg	Sodium mmol	Potassium mmol	Kcal
Liver, beef, raw	100	3 medium slices	136	5.9	7.2	135
Ham, boiled	53	1 slice	695	30.2	6.7	126
Meat loaf	100	3½ oz	653	28.4	9.6	160
Pork, leg, roast lean	45	2 medium slices	32	1.4	5.9	81
Salami	30	1 slice	540	23.5	2.6	112
Sausage, pork, links	20	1 link	192	8.3	1.4	94
Tongue, cooked	100	3½ oz	61	2.6	4.2	244

Fish

Cod, raw	100	1 medium, fillet	70	3.0	9.8	78
Cod fried in batter	147	1 fillet	448	19.5	10.4	354
Crab, boiled	100	3½ oz	850	37.0	2.4	93
Haddock, smoked	100	1 medium fillet	618	61.8	8.8	103
Herring	100	3½ oz	74	3.2	10.8	98
Lobster, boiled	334	1 (¾ lb)	210	9.1	4.6	308
Mussels, boiled	100	3½ oz	289	12.6	8.1	95
Shrimp, peeled	100	3½ oz	140	6.1	5.6	91
Sardines, canned	100	8 medium	510	22.2	14.4	311
Tuna, canned in oil	100	⅝ cup	800	34.8	7.8	197

Dairy products

Butter, salted	5	1 level tsp	41	1.78	tr	36
Butter, unsalted	5	1 level tsp	tr	tr	tr	36
Margarine, salted	5	1 level tsp	49	2.1	tr	36
Margarine, unsalted	5	1 level tsp	tr	tr	tr	36
Vegetable oil	15	1 tbsp	tr	tr	tr	135
Eggs	48	1 medium	59	2.6	1.6	78
Milk, skim	246	1 cup	128	5.6	10.5	89
Milk, low fat (2 per cent fat)	244	1 cup	122	5.3	9.6	122
Milk, whole (3.5 per cent fat)	244	1 cup	120	5.2	9.5	150
Milk, goat's	244	1 cup	83	3.6	11.3	163
Milkshake	345	1 cup	333	14.5	17.2	356
Cream, table/coffee	15	1 tbsp	6	0.3	0.5	29
Cream, whipping	15	1 tbsp	6	0.3	0.3	52
Yogurt, plain	227	1 cup, low fat	159	6.9	13.6	143
Yogurt, flavored	227	1 cup, low fat	133	5.8	11.3	231

Cheese

Blue-type	28	1 oz	390	16.7	1.8	103
Camembert-type	28	1 oz	236	10.3	0.8	84
Cheddar-type	28	1 oz	197	8.6	0.6	112
Cheese spread	28	1 oz	381	16.6	1.8	82
Cottage cheese	28	1 oz	64	0.6	0.6	30
Cream cheese	28	1 oz or 1 rounded tbsp	84	3.6	0.9	99
Edam-type	28	1 oz	270	11.7	1.4	87

	Wt (g)	Handy measure	Sodium mg	Sodium mmol	Potassium mmol	Kcal
Processed cheese	28	1 oz	318	13.8	0.6	107
Ricotta	124	½ cup	155	6.7	4.0	216
Parmesan, grated	15	1 tbsp	93	4.0	0.1	23
Pizza, tomato and cheese	65	1 small piece	455	19.8	2.2	145

Bread, cookies, crackers, cakes and desserts

Breads

	Wt (g)	Handy measure	Sodium mg	Sodium mmol	Potassium mmol	Kcal
Cornbread	45	1 piece	335	14.6	1.5	105
Wholewheat bread	23	1 slice	121	5.3	1.6	56
White bread	23	1 slice	117	5.1	0.6	62
Salt-free wholewheat bread	23	1 slice	2.3	0.1	2.3	86
Salt-free white bread	23	1 slice	2.3	0.1	1.0	93
Rye bread	23	1 slice	128	5.6	0.9	56
Bran muffin	40	1 average	179	7.8	4.4	104
Pancakes	45	1 average	209	9.1	2.8	90
Tortillas	30	1 average, 6 in diameter	33	1.4	0.1	63
Waffles	75	1 medium	356	15.5	2.8	209

Cookies, crackers

	Wt (g)	Handy measure	Sodium mg	Sodium mmol	Potassium mmol	Kcal
Chocolate chip cookie	11	1 individual cookie	38	1.7	0.3	57
Icing filled cookie	14	1 cookie	68	3.0	0.1	69
Fig bar	14	1 bar	35	1.5	0.7	50
Oatmeal raisin cookie	14	1 cookie	23	1.0	1.3	63
Peanut butter cookie	14	1 cookie	58	2.5	1.5	69
Shortbread	14	2 cookies, small	8	0.4	0.3	70
Rye wafer	7	1 wafer	62	2.7	1.1	24
Graham cracker	14	2 crackers	94	4.1	1.4	54
Wheat thins	8	2 crackers	44	1.9	—	32

Cakes and desserts

	Wt (g)	Handy measure	Sodium mg	Sodium mmol	Potassium mmol	Kcal
Apple brown betty	140	½ cup	214	9.3	3.6	211
Brownies	30	1 piece, small	75	3.3	1.5	146
Carrot cake	50	1 piece	216	9.4	1.6	173
Cheesecake, cherry	85	1 piece	98	4.3	1.9	222
Chocolate cake	50	1 piece	195	8.5	1.4	200
Chocolate sauce	39	2 tbsp	36	1.6	2.9	87
Danish, average	105	1 roll	408	17.7	1.6	360
Doughnut, raised	65	1, jelly center	70	3.0	0.6	226
Fruit cake, no icing	40	1 piece	63	2.7	5.1	152
Fruit crisp	100	3 in × 3 in portion	162	7.0	2.3	172
Fruit pie, average	160	1 piece, 3 in across	482	21.0	3.3	410
Gingerbread	50	1 piece	118	5.1	5.8	227
Ice cream, vanilla	133	1 cup	84	3.7	6.2	257
Jello	114	½ cup	33	1.4	tr	102
Milk pudding	145	¾ cup (eg, butterscotch)	644	28.0	6.1	207
Pie crust, salt added	135	⅙ crust	137	6.0	0.3	112

	Wt (g)	Handy measure	Sodium mg	Sodium mmol	Potassium mmol	Kcal
Plain sponge cake	50	1 piece	84	3.7	1.1	149
Rice pudding	145	¾ cup, with raisins	103	4.5	6.6	212

Cereals

Cereals
Bran, wheat	9	1 level tbsp	2.3	0.1	1.5	32
Corn grits, cooked	242	1 cup	tr	tr	0.7	123
Cornmeal	118	1 cup	1628	70.8	7.1	409
Flour, wholewheat	120	1 cup	4	tr	11.4	400
Flour, white, all-purpose	8	1 tbsp	tr	tr	0.2	29
Macaroni, white, boiled	140	1 cup	1	tr	2.8	207
Oatmeal, dry	28	⅓ cup	0.6	tr	2.5	111
Oatmeal, cooked with salt	177	¾ cup	1159	50.4	3.3	113
Popcorn, popped	14	1 cup	tr	tr	1.1	54
Rice, cooked, white	150	1 cup	2.3	0.1	1.1	164
Rice, cooked, brown	150	1 cup	2.3	0.1	1.8	178
Spaghetti, boiled, white	146	1 cup	tr	tr	2.9	210
Spaghetti, canned in tomato sauce	221	1 cup	955	41.5	7.8	168

Breakfast cereals
All-Bran	56	1 cup	567	24.6	13.3	129
Cornflakes	22	1 cup	216	9.4	0.7	84
Puffed wheat	14	1 cup	1	tr	1.2	53
Rice Krispies	28	1 cup	251	10.9	0.8	106
Shredded wheat	25	1 biscuit	1	tr	2.2	89
Sugar Pops	28	1 cup	63	2.8	0.5	109
Wheat flakes	30	1 cup	310	13.5	2.5	114
Breakfast bar, average	43	1 bar	219	9.5	2.9	187

Sugar, preserves, candies

Sugar, light brown	14	1 tbsp	tr	tr	tr	14
Sugar, white granulated	5	1 tsp	tr	tr	tr	16
Syrup, cane	20	1 tbsp	14	0.6	2.2	53
Molasses	20	1 tbsp	16	0.7	7.7	50
Molasses, blackstrap	20	1 tbsp	19	0.8	7.6	53
Honey	20	1 tbsp	1	tr	0.3	61
Jam, all varieties	20	1 tbsp	tr	tr	tr	55
Marmalade	20	1 tbsp	3	tr	tr	51
Caramels	28	3 pieces	76	3.3	2.2	113
Chocolate, milk	28	1 oz	26	1.1	2.8	146
Chocolate, semisweet	28	1 oz	9	0.4	1.9	148
Chocolate, filled, average	15	1	1	tr	0.4	51
Hard candy	28	6 pieces	9	0.4	tr	108

	Wt (g)	Handy measure	Sodium mg	Sodium mmol	Potassium mmol	Kcal
Jelly beans	28	10 pieces	3	tr	tr	66
Mints	28	14 small pieces	47	2.0	tr	104

Nuts

Almonds, shelled	15	12 to 15 nuts	tr	tr	2.7	90
Brazils, shelled	15	4 medium	tr	tr	2.6	97
Cashews, shelled	15	6 to 8 nuts	tr	tr	1.8	84
Chestnuts, shelled	15	2 large or 3 small	tr	tr	1.6	29
Coconut, flaked	15	2 tbsp	tr	tr	3.0	83
Filberts/hazelnuts, shelled	15	10 to 12 nuts	tr	tr	1.8	97
Peanuts, fresh shelled	100	3½ oz	tr	tr	18.5	543
Peanuts, salted	100	3½ oz	460	20.0	17.9	566
Peanut butter	15	1 tbsp	18	0.8	3.2	86
Sunflower seeds	100	3½ oz	30	1.3	23.6	560
Walnuts, shelled	8	1 tbsp, chopped	tr	tr	0.9	49

Sauces and pickles

Barbeque sauce	16	1 tbsp	130	5.6	0.7	15
Chili sauce	17	1 tbsp	228	9.9	1.6	17
Chow chow, sweet	28	1 oz	148	6.4	—	32
Dill pickle	100	1 large	1428	62.1	5.1	11
Mayonnaise	14	1 tbsp	84	3.6	0.1	101
Relish, sweet	15	1 tbsp	107	4.6	—	21
Salad dressing, French	15	1 tbsp	192	8.3	0.3	57
Salad dressing, 1000 Island	14	1 tbsp	98	4.3	0.4	70
Soy sauce	15	1 tbsp	858	37.3	1.4	11
Tomato catsup	15	1 tbsp	156	6.8	1.4	16
Tomato paste, no salt	100	3½ oz	38	1.6	22.8	82

Soups, purchased

Chicken, cream of	234	1 cup	983	42.7	2.1	117
Chicken noodle	234	1 cup	866	22.2	1.2	70
Minestrone	218	1 cup	818	35.6	7.1	87
Mushroom, cream of	218	1 cup	883	38.4	1.7	131
Onion	113	1 cup	744	32.5	0.4	38
Tomato, cream of	230	1 cup	771	33.5	6.2	104
Vegetable	218	1 cup	709	30.8	4.7	87

Miscellaneous

Accent (MSG)	5	1 level tsp	62	2.7	—	14
Baking powder, commercial	3	1 level tsp	486	21.1	tr	3
Baking powder, low sodium	3	1 level tsp	tr	tr	8.4	5
Beef broth, instant dry	17	1 level tbsp	3611	157.0	tr	30
Bouillon cube	6	1 cube	619	26.9	1.1	14
Cornstarch	10	1 tbsp	—	—	—	36
Salt	5	1 level tsp	1941	84.4	tr	0

	Wt (g)	Handy measure	Sodium mg	Sodium mmol	Potassium mmol	Kcal
Vinegar	15	1 tbsp	tr	tr	0.4	2
Yeast, active dry	8	1 tbsp	4	0.2	4.1	23

Beverages

Cocoa	6	1 tbsp	8	0.4	2.7	25
Coffee, ground, percolated or drip	236	1 cup	26	1.1	tr	2
Coffee, instant	236	1 cup	2	tr	2.2	2
Drinking chocolate	8	1 tbsp	14	tr	0.9	28
Ovaltine	21	1 serving (approximately 1 tbsp)	168	7.3	6.3	79
Tea (brewed)	236	1 cup	tr	tr	0.9	2

Soft drinks and juices

Cola	360	12 oz	22	1.0	tr	129
Grapefruit juice, unsweetened	250	1 cup	2	tr	10.4	98
Lemonade	100	½ cup	tr	tr	0.4	44
Orange soda	360	12 oz	18	0.8	0.4	167
Orange juice, unsweetened	100	½ cup	1	tr	5.1	45
Pineapple juice	100	½ cup	1	tr	3.9	55
Tomato juice	100	½ cup	200	8.7	5.8	19
Fruit drinks, powdered	28	1 oz (2 tbsp), dry	13	0.6	1.9	103

Alcoholic drinks

Ale, mild	230	8 oz	48	2.1	2.5	98
Beer (4.5 per cent alcohol by volume)	360	12 oz	25	1.1	2.3	151

Wines, sherries and aperitifs

Red, white table wine (12.2 per cent alcohol by volume)	100	1 glass (3½ oz)	5	0.5	2.4	85
Sauterne	100	1 glass (3½ oz)	6.9	0.3	2.4	84
Sherry, medium	60	1 sherry glass (2 oz)	2	tr	1.2	84
Vermouth, dry	100	1 glass (3½ oz)	4	tr	1.9	105
Dessert wine (18.8 per cent alcohol by volume)	100	1 wine glass (3½ oz)	4	tr	1.9	137

Liquor

Liquor, 70 per cent proof	45	1 jigger (1½ oz)	1	tr	tr	104

ACKNOWLEDGMENTS

I am very grateful to my wife, Christiane, who taught me how much better food is without salt and whose help, particularly with the recipes, made this book possible; and to Marie Roberts, Blood Pressure and Metabolic Unit dietitian at Charing Cross Hospital, who provided all the calculations and tables as well as much advice.

Many others in the Blood Pressure Unit at Charing Cross Hospital have helped me and I am indebted to all of them, particularly Diana Elder and Nirmala Markandu.

Lastly I am grateful to the many patients who some years ago, convinced me—much to my surprise—how easy it is to reduce salt intake and how much better food tastes without salt.

Graham MacGregor, 1984

The publishers are grateful to the following individuals and organisations for their help in the preparation of this book. Revlon Health Care (UK) for their assistance with the photographs; David Mellor Ltd, 26 James Street, WC2 for providing some of the kitchen equpiment.

The photographs were taken by Peter Myers, assisted by Neil Mersh; art direction was by Rose and Lamb Design Partnership, styling by Penny Markham and food preparation by Lisa Collard.

The diagrams were drawn by David Gifford.

INDEX

Page numbers in *italic* refer to the illustrations.

Other titles in the series

HIGH BLOOD PRESSURE
What it means for you, and how to control it
Eoin O'Brien, MD, and
Kevin O'Malley, MD

BEAT HEART DISEASE!
A cardiologist explains how you can help your heart and enjoy a healthier life
Prof Risteard Mulcahy

DON'T FORGET FIBER IN YOUR DIET
To help avoid many of our commonest diseases
Denis Burkitt, MD

ASTHMA AND HAY FEVER
How to relieve wheezing and sneezing
Allan Knight, MD

OVERCOMING ARTHRITIS
A guide to coping with stiff or aching joints
Frank Dudley Hart, MD

PSORIASIS
A guide to one of the commonest skin diseases
Prof Ronald Marks

DIABETES
A practical new guide to healthy living
Jim Anderson, MD

THE DIABETICS' DIET BOOK
A new high-fiber eating program
Jim Mann, MD, and the Oxford Dietetic Group

STRESS AND RELAXATION
Self-help ways to cope with stress and relieve nervous tension, ulcers, insomnia, migraine and high blood pressure
Jane Madders

VARICOSE VEINS
How they are treated, and what you can do to help
Harold Ellis, MD

ECZEMA AND DERMATITIS
How to cope with inflamed skin
Rona MacKie, MD

ANXIETY AND DEPRESSION
A practical guide to recovery
Robert Priest, MD

ACNE
Advice on clearing your skin
Prof Ronald Marks

OVERCOMING DYSLEXIA
A straightforward guide for families and teachers
Bevé Hornsby, PhD

EYES
Their problems and treatments
Michael Glasspool, FRCS

CONQUERING PAIN
How to overcome the discomfort of arthritis, backache, migraine, heart disease, childbirth, period pains and many other common conditions
Dr Sampson Lipton

THE DIABETICS' COOKBOOK
Delicious new recipes for entertaining and all the family
Roberta Longstaff, SRD, and Jim Mann, MD